The Passionate Spectator

POETS ON POETRY

David Lehman, General Editor
Donald Hall, Founding Editor

New titles

John Ashbery, *Selected Prose*
Annie Finch, *The Body of Poetry*
Alice Notley, *Coming After*
Charles Simic, *Memory Piano*
John Yau, *The Passionate Spectator*

Recently published

Dana Gioia, *Barrier of a Common Language*
Paul Hoover, *Fables of Representation*
Philip Larkin, *Further Requirements*
William Stafford, *The Answers Are Inside the Mountains*
Richard Tillinghast, *Poetry and What Is Real*

Also available are collections by

A. R. Ammons, Robert Bly, Philip Booth, Marianne Boruch, Hayden Carruth, Amy Clampitt, Douglas Crase, Robert Creeley, Donald Davie, Thomas M. Disch, Tess Gallagher, Linda Gregerson, Allen Grossman, Thom Gunn, Rachel Hadas, John Haines, Donald Hall, Joy Harjo, Robert Hayden, Edward Hirsch, Daniel Hoffman, Jonathan Holden, John Hollander, Andrew Hudgins, Josephine Jacobsen, Mark Jarman, Galway Kinnell, Kenneth Koch, John Koethe, Yusef Komunyakaa, Maxine Kumin, Martin Lammon (editor), Philip Larkin, David Lehman, Philip Levine, Larry Levis, John Logan, William Logan, William Matthews, William Meredith, Jane Miller, David Mura, Carol Muske, Geoffrey O'Brien, Gregory Orr, Alicia Suskin Ostriker, Ron Padgett, Marge Piercy, Anne Sexton, Karl Shapiro, Charles Simic, William Stafford, Anne Stevenson, May Swenson, James Tate, Richard Tillinghast, C. K. Williams, Alan Williamson, Charles Wright, James Wright, and Stephen Yenser

John Yau

The Passionate Spectator

ESSAYS ON ART AND POETRY

THE UNIVERSITY OF MICHIGAN PRESS
Ann Arbor

Published in the United States of America by
The University of Michigan Press
Manufactured in the United States of America
♾Printed on acid-free paper

2009 2008 2007 2006 4 3 2 1

A CIP catalog record for this book is available from the British Library.

Library of Congress Cataloging-in-Publication Data

Yau, John, 1950–
The passionate spectator : essays on art and poetry / John Yau.
p. cm. — (Poets on poetry)
ISBN-13: 978-0-472-09952-8 (alk. paper)
ISBN-10: 0-472-09952-3 (alk. paper)
ISBN-13: 978-0-472-06952-1 (pbk. : alk. paper)
ISBN-10: 0-472-06952-7 (pbk. : alk. paper)
I. Title. II. Series.

PS3575.A9Z46 2006
809.1—dc22 2006011819

Acknowledgments

Grateful acknowledgment is made to the editors, publishers, and curators who, in many cases, solicited these essays. I would particularly like to single out and thank Mary Jo Bang, Amy Cappellazzo, Hank Hine, Faye Hirsch, Joseph Lease, Eric Lorberer, Pia Müller-Tamm, and Arthur Vogelsang.

I would like to thank the Peter S. Reed Foundation and the Foundation for Contemporary Performance Art for grants that were of immense help to me during the writing and editing of this book.

For the space, time, and hospitality they provided, I would like to thank the Arcadia Summer Arts program, the Atlantic Center for the Arts, the Fine Arts Work Center (Provincetown, Massachusetts), and the Vermont Studio Center.

Finally, I would like to thank David Lehman, whose editorial suggestions inspired me to rethink and reshape this manuscript.

Contents

Passionate Spectator

On Frank O'Hara's Art Criticism

> You know how
> I feel about painters. I sometimes think poetry
> only describes.
>
> —Frank O'Hara

I.

Frank O'Hara refused to play it safe in terms of either poetry or art. He didn't think that being a poet had to do with getting published and having a career, and while he took the role of curator seriously, it wasn't a position he set his sights on. A careerist, that is to say one who both supports and accommodates the status quo, would have done things much differently than O'Hara. In 1954, wearing only army boots, he posed nude for a painting by Larry Rivers and drawings by Fairfield Porter. In Rivers's notorious painting *O'Hara Nude with Boots,* as well as in the lesser-known drawings by Porter, O'Hara is standing in a mock-heroic pose. With his hands folded on top of his head, he flaunts himself. This doesn't strike us as the kind of gesture we would associate with a curator. In fact, it might strike many as unseemly.

O'Hara's pose isn't coy. Unembarrassed about his body, he has literally put himself on display. He has come out of the closet in a way that is both sly and in your face. Through it all, you can hear him daring the viewer: It's up to you how you choose to read this position. For if you don't like this or it offends your delicate sensibilities, that's your tough luck, because,

From *Rain Taxi,* vol. 5, no. 4 (Winter 2000–2001).

while you don't have to live with me, I have to live with myself every day.

Even today, half a century later, one is still struck by O'Hara's ability to be simultaneously vulnerable, outrageous, and self-mocking. He is self-possessed and provocative, distanced and theatrical. Aware that he was exposing more than just his body, which was already a defiant gesture in the 1950s, O'Hara always seemed ready to test just exactly how far he could go before the world closed and barred its doors to him. That it never did completely close them while he was alive is a testament to his self-assurance and uncanny ability to negotiate the different scenes in which he moved.

If, in today's art world, O'Hara's theatrical gesture has come to seem tame, it is still hardly the kind of early career move you would expect from a person who, in 1960, became an assistant curator in the Department of Painting and Sculpture at the Museum of Modern Art. An artist would have been more likely to pose as O'Hara did, but certainly not a curator. Can you imagine someone wanting to be hired by a major museum deciding to pose nude, exposing himself for all to see? O'Hara's most egregious sin is his intimacy. Curators aren't supposed to be involved in art making, they are paid to keep their distance and observe. They aren't supposed to remove their clothes in front of artists. How could they maintain their objectivity?[1]

By his mid-twenties, O'Hara seems to have known how to live in the present, as well as test its capacity to absorb his presence. He was sustained by the present, and its daily turbulence, rather than by an idea about the future and his place in it. You could say that O'Hara lived a bohemian life, but that doesn't begin to tell the full story. There is no such thing as a bohemian curator. He was able to juggle many possibilities at once. When he died in 1966, at forty, his present was hardly one smooth continuum. It consisted of many abutting but not necessarily overlapping worlds. It included the internal workings of the Museum of Modern Art, the New York art world, the international art scene, the uptown and downtown literary scenes, the realm of small presses and avant-garde writing, and their scattered centers of activity. Because O'Hara was gay, it is likely that he lived in different and separate worlds for much, if not all his life. Living multiple lives, however, is hardly uncommon. We all do it to some degree.

What is remarkable is that O'Hara appears to have lived in all of them at full throttle. And what is evident in Rivers's painting, Porter's drawings, and O'Hara's early poetry is that he didn't try to hide his homosexuality. On a fundamental level, he was unabashed about who he was. It is O'Hara's brilliant enthusiasm that one encounters in his art criticism; its energetic mixture of the charming and the outlandish distinguishes his writing from most nearly everyone else's. It is these very aspects of his writing, and the fact that he was neither an art historian nor someone who developed a theoretical paradigm, which have repeatedly been held against him.

Except for a small group of devoted readers, O'Hara wasn't taken seriously as a poet until after the posthumous publication of *The Collected Poems,* with Rivers's portrait as the cover for the first edition.[2] With this and subsequent publications of his poetry and art criticism, O'Hara was discovered by academia and, more importantly, by new generations of readers.[3] While many have written about O'Hara's relationship with artists, most notably Marjorie Perloff, his art criticism is still regarded as marginal, at best.[4]

While I am not proposing that O'Hara's reviews and essays are as important as those of the art historian Leo Steinberg, who, in the 1960s, was one of the few truly independent observers of contemporary art, I do think it is time to reconsider both his stance and his art criticism. For although O'Hara's writing is often provocatively associational, and Steinberg's is always passionately analytical, they share a tough-minded independence, as well as a refusal to follow others or be part of the status quo. They possess an enormous empathy toward art and artists and are driven by what they see, rather than by a preexisting theory. This alone makes O'Hara and Steinberg rather unique figures.

II.

O'Hara's ability to live in, as well as respond to, the present sets him apart from his contemporary Clement Greenberg, the influential formalist critic, and differentiates him from later figures such as William Rubin, who was the director of the Department of Painting and Sculpture at the Museum of Modern Art from 1973 to '88. Greenberg didn't live in the present, but in the narrative he constructed about the progress of art. Over time, he refined and developed a narrow set of criteria. During his tenure at the museum, Rubin, like Greenberg, applied a historicist narrative that privileged a narrow set of formal issues over all else. Derived in part from Greenberg's, Rubin's criteria seemed designed to apply only to Frank Stella, to whom he gave two MOMA-sanctioned retrospectives.

O'Hara looked at art from a very different vantage point, one that was less protected, more open. Instead of approaching art with a theory, whose primary purpose is to aid the critic in establishing a hierarchy of verifiable values, he lived as a *flaneur,* which means he tried to live in the now as completely as possible. It is not that O'Hara ignored or rejected the past or that he didn't have values. Rather, he didn't contextualize the present according to a preestablished framework.

A true *flaneur* doesn't believe either that he or she is superior to anyone else or that intelligence saves one from the world and its vagaries. In fact, a *flaneur* knows intelligence provides no protection and small defense in the end. One is always vulnerable and, in that sense, naked. To be a *flaneur* is to reject a vantage point and any trace of omniscience in favor of being open. Walt Whitman was our first *flaneur.* O'Hara's home was the streets of Manhattan.

Charles Baudelaire, who originated the term *flaneur,* wrote:

> The crowd is his element, as the air is that of birds and water of fishes. His passions and his profession are to become one flesh with the crowd. For the perfect *flaneur,* for the passionate spectator, it is an immense joy to set up house in the heart of the multitude, amid the ebb and flow of movement, in the midst of the fugitive and infinite. To be away from home and yet to feel oneself everywhere at home; to see the world, to be at the center of the world, and yet to remain hidden from the world—such are a few of these slightest pleasures of those independent, passionate, impartial natures that the tongue can but clumsily define. The spectator is a *prince* who everywhere

> rejoices in his incognito. The lover of life makes the whole world his family, just like the lover of the fair sex who builds up his family from all the beautiful women that he has ever found, or that are—or are not—to be found, or the lover of pictures who lives in a magical society of dreams painted on canvas. Thus the lover of universal life enters into the crowd as though it were an immense reservoir of electrical energy.[5]

In "Art Chronicle" (1962), O'Hara makes this observation about "ABSTRACT EXPRESSIONISTS AND IMAGISTS," a large survey exhibition at the Guggenheim Museum:

> What does happen in the show, without disturbing anyone's reputation, is a shift in the emphasis of who is doing the interesting work: some artists maintain their vitality, others look terribly dull. Younger artists zoom to the fore, all on the fore-admitted basis of one recent work, so no images are toppled permanently. This is a perfectly fair thing to have happen and gives the show a free-wheeling accuracy. This is all living art and the show reflects the living situation: just as Al Held and Joan Mitchell and Philip Guston will absorb the imagination one season, so do Michael Goldberg and Robert Motherwell and Franz Kline another. It depends on what you see and when it's shown and it keeps you fresh for looking and for the excitement of art. A lot of people would like to see art dead and sure, but you don't see them up at The Cloisters reading Latin.[6]

In the very next paragraph, O'Hara writes:

> The present show also, precisely because it is made up of recent works, reflects another very human situation: the relation between artists of a given tendency is frequently very close. Why this should be a matter of concern to anyone but the artists themselves is beyond me, since the alternative to this fortuitous happening are blindness or hypocrisy. Nevertheless, the viewer should make more distinctions than the artist, he has time and room for it, he is merely looking and experiencing, where the artist is creating something, whether in his own or another's image, no small feat in either case.[7]

Aligning himself with artists, rather than viewers (all of whom are critics), O'Hara writes: "Nevertheless, the viewer should make more distinctions than the artist, he has time and room for it, he is merely looking and experiencing, where the artist is creating something, whether in his own or another's image, no small feat in either case." This was a radical position in O'Hara's lifetime, and it continues to be so now, because it makes the viewer responsible. O'Hara doesn't believe that being content to recognize similarities is enough, and admonishes the viewer to notice distinctions and register differences, to be active and engaged. Looking requires "time." No matter how intelligent and sophisticated we happen to be, and no matter how familiar we think we are with contemporary art, "looking and experiencing" are required at all times. It might seem like the painting was made quickly, but that doesn't mean we should be satisfied with glancing at it.

In giving an overview of the exhibition, O'Hara observes, "This is all living art and the show reflects the living situation." In the next paragraph, and echoing his awareness of paintings of a "given tendency" looking alike, he uses the phrase "very human situation." This is the context he tries to apply to his experience of art; it is a "living" and "human situation." Even though his role is that of a critic, O'Hara doesn't see himself as separate from, or worse, above, the situation. For him, the "living situation" means that certain artists "can absorb the imagination one season," that artists from different generations and tendencies aren't viewed hierarchically, and that the individual, whom Baudelaire called the "passionate spectator," must always be open to experience itself, as he (or she) makes his (or her) way through a "free-wheeling" reality.

O'Hara's critical stance runs counter to what many believe an art critic, curator, or, more recently, cultural theorist should do, which is possess and continually refine a set of standards which is brought to bear on the situation. By contrast, O'Hara felt that the viewer must always be alert in a reality that is contingent and constantly changing. Literally speaking, he has no fixed paradigm, no previously established model by which to judge art. If anything, O'Hara makes no distinction between his critical stance and the writing of poetry, where, as he said, "You have to go on your nerve alone." In trying to maintain his openness, O'Hara achieves what Wallace Stevens challenges all of us to do: "Live in the world but outside of existing conceptions of it." You can't get much more radical than that, or much more exposed.

The "you" O'Hara uses ("you don't see them up at The Cloisters reading Latin.") is the kind of intimate address one is used to finding in letters or postcards sent by a friend. The "you" most critics use feels more general than specific; it is addressed to an audience rather than to the solitary individual. O'Hara was always conscious that solitariness is what all of us have in common. When we read O'Hara's writing, whether poetry or criticism, we are unique and alone; each of us is getting a letter from a friend.

At the end of "Art Chronicle," O'Hara does something almost no one writing about art since then would dream of doing; he juxtaposes two very different artists working in very different ways, in this case Norman Bluhm and Jasper Johns, in order to point out an unlikely affinity, Jackson Pollock:

> A great deal has been written about the influence of Pollock, but that is all about the *look,* the technique which is best known (Pollock had several). Bluhm is the only artist working in the idiom of Abstract Expressionism who has a spirit similar to that of Pollock, which is to say that he is *out*—beyond beauty, beyond composition, beyond the old-fashioned kind of pictorial ambition. And Jasper Johns is somehow in this area, a very misunderstood artist, whose art seems to many something easily assimilable and understood, but Johns is one of the most mysterious artists of our time, an artist whose work is *not* formal, in the sense that it is understood and expounded. He has the experience, which may or may not be unfortunate for him, of seeing his paintings greeted with delight because the images are recognizable when they are filled with pain.[8]

The point on which O'Hara connects Pollock, Bluhm, and Johns is their "spirit" or desire to make work that is "beyond beauty, beyond composition, beyond the old-fashioned kind of pictorial ambition." In order to connect these three disparate figures, each of whom belongs to a different generation,[9]

O'Hara separates Pollock's technique from his ambition. As O'Hara points out, Pollock "had several" techniques. The dripping of paint, and the seeming removal of his hand in the act of painting, is neither the only technique he developed nor the only option one has if one is to make radical art.

As O'Hara sees it, Pollock's techniques had helped make an idiom, not a style or method one should practice. He also recognizes that Johns, while working in a very different way than Pollock, is somehow in the same "area," a place that is "beyond" the old, assimilated standards. O'Hara's use of "area," which defines space rather than time, suggests that he would not have agreed with those critics who, within in a few years, would propose that Pop art, particularly the work of Andy Warhol and Roy Lichtenstein, had eclipsed Abstract Expressionism. The "living situation" was not a linear, historical progression; it was not about one style replacing another.

It also is very likely that O'Hara wouldn't have gone along with the more recent, widely held view that proposes that Johns and Robert Rauschenberg are still tied to Abstract Expressionism, while Warhol marks a historical break between one way of thinking about painting and another. This is too neat a sequence for someone engaged with a "free-wheeling reality." In fact, I believe O'Hara would have recognized that after Pollock, many possibilities could exist simultaneously, and he wouldn't have necessarily privileged one over another. If critics accept that view, the job of looking suddenly gets a lot harder.

O'Hara concludes "Art Chronicle" with: "Johns's business is to resist desire, Bluhm unconsciously inspires it. But more, of course, must be thought about both." By rejecting closure, not to mention sweeping conclusions, in favor of what he earlier called "the living situation," he defers his chance to have the last word, make a grand or inclusive summation. There is a humbleness in O'Hara that we don't associate with critics.

In writing about Johns, O'Hara offers one reason why he rejected Greenberg's brand of formalism: "Johns is . . . an artist whose work is *not* formal, in the sense that it is understood and expounded." He understood that formalism, even when it was stretched to accommodate Johns, as it was by a generation of younger critics who emphasized the flatness of the artist's choice of motifs (American flag, target), still failed to get at the meaning of his paintings. This was because these critics believed that an elegantly economical solution to a formal issue (the flatness of the painting) was proof of the artist's ambition. Such thinking is solipsistic, a way of not engaging with the work itself.

In contrast, O'Hara realized that Johns didn't choose the American flag because it was flat; that there were other reasons it was the focus of his paintings. In recognizing that technique could transform matter (paint), as well as subject (American flag), into an experience that was meaningful rather than purely aesthetic, he recognized that Johns's work had to be seen with fresh eyes. He also had the insight that Johns's work had to do with "pain," a loaded word, particularly in the art world, which emphasizes surface. O'Hara's use of "pain" distinguishes Johns's work from formal irony, which is how his work was seen in the 1960s, as well as from the hermetic, which is how his work has been routinely described since the 1970s. Art isn't about the *"look,"* as O'Hara points out. It never has been.

In seeing "pain" as the possible subject of Johns's work, O'Hara shares something with Leo Steinberg, whose 1962 essay "Jasper Johns, The First Seven Years of His Art" still stands out among the countless pages written on Johns.[10] Written with fresh eyes, which is to say without assumptions or agendas, Steinberg's essay is a prolonged and insightful look at the artist's work. Had O'Hara had the time to write a longer piece on Johns, I believe he also would have approached his work without an agenda, and may have written something memorable.

In addition to refusing to write about artists hierarchically in terms of style or generation, O'Hara doesn't use labels to contain or generalize. He doesn't describe Mitchell, Goldberg, and Bluhm as "second-generation Abstract Expressionists." Based on his understanding that Abstract Expressionism is an idiom, he links Bluhm and Pollock, which is remarkably prescient, given the subsequent trajectory of Bluhm's painting, particularly his interest in synthesizing the ornamental with infinite space, his transformation of the Abstract Expressionist idiom into a more inclusive possibility, something O'Hara never lived to see.

O'Hara's respect for art and artists is so real and focused, it took this reader a while to realize that his essay is equally remarkable for what he doesn't do in it; he never uses one artist to beat up another. By refusing to pit two artists or styles against each other, a fight that is always fixed, O'Hara doesn't fulfill the familiar role of tastemaker that we have come to associate with art critics. He neither views art from an elevated vantage point nor presents himself as an omniscient narrator or puppet master who defines art according to a narrative he himself has created. Fiction and power of this kind never interested O'Hara, while art and truth, however provisional and fleeting, always did.

If you happen to think that O'Hara's writing about art complements his poetry, which I do, then you are left wishing that he had been able, on other occasions, to write at length on Bluhm and Johns, both of whom he knew and championed. In one of O'Hara's few extended pieces of art writing, *Jackson Pollock,* the reader senses what O'Hara might have done had he lived.[11] I don't think it is too much to say that O'Hara's death caused a rupture in the art world's thinking that has never been entirely healed.

O'Hara, who had been a firsthand observer of the latter half of Pollock's career, stresses that his "drip" paintings have "no need for the mediation of metaphor or symbol." Addressing the issue of scale in tandem with his technique of dripping, O'Hara writes:

> This is a drastic innovation hitherto unanticipated, even in the mural-size works of Picasso and Matisse. No wonder, then, that when these paintings were first shown in the Betty Parsons Gallery the impression was one of inexplicable violence and savagery. They seemed about to engulf one. This violence, however, was not an intrinsic quality of the paintings, but a response to Pollock's violation of our ingrained assumptions regarding scale. So impressively had Pollock expounded his insight into the qualities dormant in the use of scale that when seen only a few years later at the Janis Gallery or in The Museum of Modern Art the violence had been transmuted into a powerful personal lyricism. The paintings had not changed, but the world around them had.[12]

In pointing out that the world, rather than Pollock's paintings, had changed, O'Hara didn't separate art from life. This is in keeping with his descriptive term "the living situation" which he used a few years later.

In contrast to almost every accepted reading of Pollock's career, O'Hara neither privileges his abstract "drip" paintings (1947–50) over the rest of his oeuvre, nor does he see the work the artist subsequently did as evidence that he was in decline. As O'Hara understands it, each phase in Pollock's career is part of the story, as well as tells a story. Thus, despite the fact that Pollock is dead, we still do not know how all the stories turn out. This is a viewpoint that I think should be seriously reconsidered,[13] if only to help us remember that there is more to art than the art-historical view of it as "dead and sure."

In writing about the paintings Pollock did in the last years of his life, particularly the black-and-white figurative works from 1951–52, O'Hara observes: "Giving up all that he had conquered in the previous period, Pollock reconfronted himself with the crisis of figuration and achieved remarkable things."[14] Compare O'Hara's view of Pollock with Kirk Varnedoe's appraisal:

> Pollock had, in essence, one great, overpowering idea. It was an edgy proposition hardly guaranteed to produce anything worthy, but he turned out to be ideally and uniquely equipped to push it beyond its apparent limitations. It came to him at the end of 1946, produced some of the most inexhaustible artworks of the century over almost four years, and then was over as abruptly as it had begun.[15]

This is what O'Hara writes less than three years after Pollock died:

> Much has been written about Pollock's difficulties in the last three years of his life, and more has been spoken. The works accomplished in these years, if created by anyone else, would have been astonishing. But for Pollock, who had incited in himself, and won, a revolution in three years (1947–50), it was not enough. This attitude has continued to obscure the qualities of some of these works, for in *Blue Poles,* he gave us one of the great masterpieces of Western art, and in *The Deep,* a work which contemporary aesthetic conjecture had cried out for. *Blue Poles* is our *Raft of the Medusa* and our *Embarkation*

> *for Cythera* in one. I say *our,* because it is the drama of the American conscience, lavish, bountiful, and rigid. It contains everything within itself, begging no quarter: a world of sentiment implied, but denied; a map of sensual freedom, fenced; a careening licentiousness, guarded by eight totems native to its origins (*There Were Seven in Eight*). What is expressed here is not only basic to his work as a whole, but it is final.[16]

Varnedoe focuses his attention on technique, while O'Hara directs our attention to the whole range of art. While it is understandable that one might think that O'Hara's writings are both excessive and impressionistic, and that he is contributing to the myth surrounding the artist, it should be pointed out that in this paragraph, as elsewhere in his monograph, he makes all of his associations based on looking at the paintings. More importantly, O'Hara doesn't suggest that Pollock had "one great, overpowering idea," which in the end trivializes both the artist and his work. And while he knew the artist personally, he neither refers to any of the myths surrounding him, nor does he attempt to add to them. Not only does O'Hara keep his distance from the myths surrounding Pollock, but he never includes an anecdote about some moment they shared.

In assessing what the artist did after the "drip" paintings, O'Hara does more than simply go against what many other critics and historians have agreed upon since shortly after Pollock died, which is that his death and precipitous decline as an artist coincided. In stark contrast to the belief that it "was over as abruptly as it began," O'Hara keeps the door open to the future without conjecturing about what might or should happen there, as well as implicitly suggests that the artist's death does not mark the end of a possibility.

At the same time, by pointing out that the works Pollock did after 1950 would have been "astonishing" if they had been done by someone else, O'Hara raises two issues. First, how much have we the right to ask from any artist? Second, if we look at an artist's oeuvre hierarchically, mustn't we admit that we are burdening that artist with our idea of who he or she is and are being implicitly proscriptive about what that artist should have done? In both cases, the relationship between viewer and artist is deeply antagonistic. It amounts to the viewer looking at artists and their work from a position of superiority, and with perfect hindsight. Who can survive such scrutiny?

O'Hara knew that art doesn't solve a problem forever, that each answer it provides produces more unexpected questions. Without making grandiose claims for the paintings he did after the "drip" paintings, he does emphasize that Pollock "achieved remarkable things." He goes on to observe: "The wonderful draftsmanship of the early drawings and the 'drip' period is here brought to bear on heads and figures of nightmarish variety and semblance."[17] By using the term "draftsmanship" to connect "early drawings" and the "drip" period to the figurative paintings from 1951–52, O'Hara challenges the notion that Pollock stopped drawing in paint when he invented the technique of dripping. He didn't stop drawing; he invented a new way of drawing in paint, which made possible other ways of applying paint to the surface. After Pollock's breakthrough, drawing didn't require the hand to be used, as it had been since the Renaissance. In stating that Pollock didn't return to figuration, but "reconfronted himself with the crisis of figuration," O'Hara reminds us that the "drip" paintings aren't proof that abstraction had superseded figuration once and for all. Certainly, Johns's "flag" paintings made the supposed conflict between abstraction and figuration a moot point.

In writing that "*Blue Poles* is our *Raft of the Medusa* and our *Embarkation of Cythera* in one," O'Hara makes an association that is both perfectly fitting and, I would propose, completely in keeping with his belief in the "living situation," particularly if you understand that he means American culture, and not just the narrow confines of the art world. It matters little whoever was the initial audience, because art was made for, and to exist in, culture. O'Hara's association isn't as wild as we might initially think once we take into account that both Gericault and Watteau died before they were forty, one from injuries incurred while riding a horse, the other from tuberculosis. Add to this the fact that Gericault depicts the raft so close to the foreground that the viewer feels like a participant in a drama which has no heroes or message, a horrific scene, which is not presided over by any divine spirit. It is a view of suffering in which there is no evidence of hope.

Meanwhile, the subject of Watteau's painting is the travel to the temple of Love. However, as a number of art historians have pointed out, there is a narrative inconsistency to Watteau's otherwise acknowledged masterpiece, which is that we do not know if the travellers are preparing to go to, or about to leave, the island. Unable to figure out the artist's exact intentions, we are perplexed as to how to read the painting. And yet this perplexity doesn't prevent us from recognizing that *Embarkation for Cythera* is a masterpiece. A perfect painting isn't necessarily a great painting, and, as O'Hara suggests, a great painting isn't necessarily perfect.

O'Hara's association reminds us that Pollock shares something with these two painters; they all died young. Thus, the three paintings he connects are singular works in their rather brief careers. Once we recognize that O'Hara's associations aren't metaphorical but definitive, we see what he is getting at. Both paintings he cites are deeply personal visions of hope and disillusionment, with neither one quite winning out. And yet, with both paintings, we never feel that the artist is being overtly autobiographical. What is evident is that Gericault focuses on death and torment, bodily suffering, while Watteau focuses on the transitoriness of love and unfulfillable dreams. There is, to use a word the poet will use about Johns's art, "pain" in these three paintings. O'Hara never stops to draw these parallels out because he assumes that we will know what he is talking about, that is how much faith he has in his reader.

After declaring that "*Blue Poles* is our *Raft of Medusa* and our *Embarkation for Cythera* in one," O'Hara shifts his attention from painting to culture, and states that *Blue Poles* "is the drama of the American conscience, lavish, bountiful, and rigid." Instead of seeing *Blue Poles* within the context of art history, and whatever narrative one brings to bear on such an experience, O'Hara locates Pollock's paintings within culture and "the drama of the American conscience." By connecting art to culture, O'Hara reveals his belief that, among other things, American art contributes to the ongoing, often contentious argument about what it means to be an American.

What is the culture we are constructing? What does our art reveal about us? In *Blue Poles,* the viewer encounters a vision of "sentiment implied, but denied; a map of sensual freedom, fenced; a careening licentiousness, guarded by eight totems native to its origins (*There Were Seven in Eight*)." As O'Hara sees it, *Blue Poles* is both a final statement about the artist's work and a telling vision of America's conscience. The freedom the artist had gained in his "drip" paintings wasn't boundless, but "fenced." It is something that Pollock both understood and faced in his work, and then, as O'Hara argues, he moved on. He wasn't in decline; he was trying to begin again when he died in a car accident.

III.

For O'Hara, art is a catalyst to, as well as a crucial component of, our understanding of the "living situation." It is never about technique or high and low. It is never meant to be a form of entertainment or a distraction. Whether it is accepted or understood by mainstream culture or not is of little importance. And yet, instead of becoming discouraged or cynical about art's impotence, O'Hara believed that art is always about culture, and its constant formation; at its best, it reveals something about ourselves that we might not necessarily want to see, much less know. It is up to us to experience art, to engage and believe in its power.

NOTES

1. For a recent and very different presentation of the curator, see Piotr Uhlanski, *Untitled (GingerAss)*, 2002, *Artforum* (Sept. 2003): pp. 102–4. The project includes a double-page spread of Uhlanski's tightly cropped photograph of a naked woman's buttocks against a red background, and the essay "Totally My Ass," by Alison M. Gingeras, a curator at the Centre Pompidou, Paris. According to Gingeras: "It is not an art project inserted in the magazine on the invitation of *Artforum*. A museum or gallery did not purchase this space. This is an advertisement paid for by the artist. Money buys visibility. Visibility caters to ego. Publication of this picture displaces it from a wall to a double page spread (closer to porn). This text ensures that my identity as the sitter is exposed. Without leaving it to gossip, it divulges a charged liaison—

potentially beneficially for the artist, problematic for the curator." The most obvious difference, and there are many, is that O'Hara posed before he was a curator, while Gingeras posed after she became one. One faced forward, the other didn't.

2. Frank O'Hara, *The Collected Poems of Frank O'Hara,* ed. Donald M. Allen (New York: Knopf, 1971).

3. Frank O'Hara, *Art Chronicles 1954–66,* 2d ed. (1975; New York: George Braziller, 1990); *Early Writing,* ed. Donald M. Allen (Bolinas, CA: Grey Fox, 1977); *Poems Retrieved,* ed. Donald M. Allen (San Francisco: Grey Fox, 1996).

4. Marjorie Perloff, *Frank O'Hara: Poet among Painters* (New York: George Braziller, 1977).

5. Charles Baudelaire, *The Painter of Modern Life and Other Essays,* trans. and ed. Jonathan Mayne (London: Phaidon Press, 1964; rpt., New York: Da Capo Press, 1986), p. 9.

6. O'Hara, *Art Chronicles,* p. 5; "Art Chronicle" originally appeared in *Kulchur* (Summer 1962).

7. O'Hara, *Art Chronicles,* p. 5.

8. O'Hara, *Art Chronicles,* pp. 9–10.

9. Jackson Pollock (1912–56), Norman Bluhm (1920–99), Jasper Johns (1930).

10. See Leo Steinberg, "Jasper Johns, The First Seven Years of His Art," in *Other Criteria: Confrontations with Twentieth-Century Art* (New York: Oxford University Press, 1972).

11. Frank O'Hara, *Jackson Pollock* (New York: George Braziller, 1959), p. 29. This was reprinted in its entirety in *Art Chronicles;* the quote is from p. 35. Subsequently, all citations will refer to *Art Chronicles,* which is still in print.

12. O'Hara, *Art Chronicles,* p. 35.

13. Kirk Varnedoe with Pepe Karmel, *Jackson Pollock,* exhibition catalog (New York: Museum of Modern Art, 1998). The catalog accompanied the retrospective of Pollock that Varnedoe curated. In his essay, Varnedoe finds no reason to cite O'Hara. Among Varnedoe's footnotes, the fourth entry reads: "Already in 1967, reflecting on the Pollock retrospective at the Museum of Modern Art, Henry Seldis observed, 'Much of Pollock that seemed so savagely violent when we first encountered it twenty years ago and led to an enormous, often spurious myth surrounding the man and his work, now emerges, little more than ten years after his death, as a gutsy lyricism that is not without a sense of celebration along with echoes of pain and frustration." Nearly a decade earlier, O'Hara had pointed out that the perception of Pollock's works had changed, because the world in which they were seen

had changed. In fact, O'Hara had anticipated each of Seldis's points by nearly a decade.

14. O'Hara, *Art Chronicles,* p. 35

15. See Varnedoe, "Comet Jackson Pollock's Life and Work," in Varnedoe and Karmel, *Jackson Pollock,* p. 62.

16. O'Hara, *Art Chronicles,* pp. 36–37.

17. O'Hara, *Art Chronicles,* p. 36.

At the Movies with Weldon Kees and Frank O'Hara

I.

Weldon Kees (1914–55) was nearly a teenager living in Nebraska when Frank O'Hara (1926–66) was born in Massachusetts. They both moved to Manhattan, and worked in the art world. Kees, however, ended up hating its winters and moved to California, while O'Hara, whose first book was *A City Winter, and Other Poems* (1952), is a central figure in the "New York School" of poets. New York was O'Hara's city more than any other postwar poet's. Who else could so offhandedly transform the city skyline into a musical?

> How funny you are today New York
> like Ginger Rogers in *Springtime*
> and St. Bridget's steeple leaning a little to the left
>
> —"Steps"

Although separated by more than a decade, and associated with different literary tendencies, Kees and O'Hara loved the movies, modern art, and all kinds of music. They found popular culture exciting and vivacious, and they hated pretense. Both died young.

Kees was forty-one when he left his car on the approach to the Golden Gate Bridge. His body was never found, and he was never heard from again. Because he vanished into thin air, rumors and sightings persisted for years, but nothing concrete was

From *American Poetry Review* 34, no. 5 (Sept.–Oct. 2005).

ever proven. Adrian Wilson had just published Kees's third and last book of poems, *Poems 1947–1954* (1954), in San Francisco. But the bulk of his writing, including poems, plays, short stories, a novel, and numerous reviews of art, music, and literature, remained either uncollected or unpublished the day he disappeared. It was July 18, 1955, and the *New Republic* had just printed his review "How to Be Happy: Installment 1053."

Kees's suicide is consistent with his poetry. He had deep friendships, but, as his poems make clear, he always felt utterly alone. In his isolation, he found neither solace nor redemption. He was like a house with only three walls, constantly battered by the weather of his interior and exterior circumstances. Death became the only release from his otherwise intolerable situation. In this regard, Kees followed Hart Crane (1899–1932), and, in turn, was followed by Lew Welch (1926–71). Crane jumped off the bow of the *Orizaba,* and Welch walked into the woods one day, disappearing without a trace. Life haunted these three men, and art couldn't save them. For different reasons, they didn't want their bodies to be found.

A little more than a decade after Kees vanished, Frank O'Hara was struck by a beach buggy on Fire Island. He died the following evening, on July 25, 1966, at the age of forty. O'Hara was a prolific poet who had published a few slim volumes during his lifetime, and his posthumously published *Collected Poems* contains over five hundred poems, including a significant number of long poems. There are three selections of his criticism available, as well as a biography, *City Poet: The Life and Times of Frank O'Hara,* by Brad Gooch (1993). By contrast, Kees's *Collected Poems* contains a little more than one hundred poems, almost all of them less than fifty lines. Both men wrote many letters, and carried on intense correspondences, but only Kees's have been published, in *Weldon Kees and the Midcentury Generation: Letters, 1935–1955* (1986, edited by Robert E. Knoll). There is also a biography of Kees, *Vanished Act: The Life and Art of Weldon Kees,* by James Reidel (2003), and a selection of his critical writings is collected in *Reviews and Essays: 1936–1955* (1988). The CD *Holiday Rag* has seventeen songs by Kees, who plays the piano, accompanied by his friend Bob Helm on clarinet and washboard (1998). Finally, we also have Kees's abstract paintings and drawings, done in the early years of Abstract Expressionism. There is, however, no catalogue raisonné or monograph documenting his artwork. While it is clear that Kees was accomplished in many different art forms, including poetry, fiction, music, and painting, I don't think this is just evidence of his restless genius. I also think that none of these forms gave him the solace he needed, and that he felt that each had failed him in some profound way. Suicide is narcissistic.

Kees became a cult figure after he died; O'Hara was a cult figure during his lifetime. After the publication of his *Collected Poems,* O'Hara was reevaluated by academia and became the subject of a full-length biography. In death, the literary establishment accepted him, whereas in life he was routinely dismissed as a cult poet writing for a small, jaded audience.[1] Part of this dismissal was predicated on the fact that O'Hara was insouciant, campy, and openly gay.

Though Kees and O'Hara had much in common, I have found no evidence that the two men ever met. It is likely that O'Hara read Kees's poetry, but he never commented upon it publicly.[2] And he wrote poems in praise of a number of poets of the previous generation, such as David Schubert and John Wheelwright, whom few of his literary contemporaries read. Although from different generations, they shared, for somewhat different reasons, a strong dislike for the East Coast literary establishment, particularly as it revolved around Robert Lowell.[3] They had much larger interests, and were neither careerists nor academics.

They were both passionate about popular culture, and their love for music extended across racial lines. Kees played jazz piano, wrote lyrics, composed tunes, and wrote an appreciation of Fats Waller for *Time* in 1943, when Waller was hardly fashionable. O'Hara studied classical music and played the piano. He wrote a moving elegy for the jazz singer Billie Holliday, "The Day Lady Died," as well as many poems in praise of Rachmaninoff. Kees was anti-heroic, while O'Hara was mock-heroic. They could be darkly sardonic, though the difference between O'Hara's self-mockery and what Dana Gioia calls Kees's "cosmic pessimism" is finally telling.

As his early poem "For My Daughter" makes evident, Kees couldn't find redemption in either poetry or life:

Looking into my daughter's eyes I read
Beneath the innocence of morning flesh
Concealed, hintings of death she does not heed.
Coldest of winds have blown this hair, and mesh
Of seaweed snarled these miniatures of hands;
The night's slow poison, tolerant and bland,
Has moved her blood. Parched years that I have seen
That may be hers appear: foul, lingering
Death in certain war, the slim legs green.
Or, fed on hate, she relishes the stings
Of others' agony; perhaps the cruel
Bride of a syphilitic or a fool.
These speculations sour in the sun.
I have no daughter. I desire none.

A fourteen-line poem that ends in a rhymed couplet, Kees's sonnet overturns one's expectations of what constitutes a sonnet. The poem begins—the reader innocently thinks—with a father looking at his young daughter and imagining her future; it is a traditional literary subject. However, what Kees's poem becomes is a list of the banal horrors that might befall his daughter ("Coldest of winds have blown this hair"). "Certain war," Kees writes, convinced that doom awaits humankind. By this time, the reader has been pulled into a vision of utter hopelessness. The loss of innocence is not only inevitable but also both traumatic and devastating.

As Kees methodically adds each grim speculation to the poem, he squeezes out any belief we might have about the goodness of the future until nothing but his grotesque imagining is left for us to ponder. A claustrophobic, all-encompassing atmosphere of utter darkness takes over the poem. Imagination, we learn at the end of the poem, not only leads the poet downward but also keeps him isolated from others. By the twelfth line ("bride of a syphilitic or a fool"), Kees's imagination has reached a cul-de-sac, which leaves the reader wondering what more will befall the hapless young daughter. Kees has reached a point in his logic where he is bordering on parody, but refuses to enter that realm. Instead, the poet admits, "These speculations sour in the sun." At this point the reader thinks that the poem might begin to consider a better future. Instead, Kees concludes: "I have no daughter. I desire none." Instead of celebrating either fatherhood or the future, the poet betrays all our expectations with these two short, insistently declarative sentences. Beneath this betrayal, the reader senses that the poet is cut off from all other human beings, as well as from any hope that the future will be better.

Kees turns the sonnet's concluding statement into both a revelation and a rejection of a traditional literary subject. What comfort, his poem asks us, did we expect to find when reading this work? Even while the reader believes that the poem is about a father's inability to protect his daughter from the vagaries of life, there is still a sense that the poet is going to make a disclosure. But Kees's disclosure jars us; it's disquieting not only because of what it says but also because of its chilling, life-denying glee.

The pacing is cinematic; the poet doesn't allow any detail to become the focus of the reader's attention. Like a movie by the Russians Vertov or Eisenstein, the poem is a montage of images, which shifts without pause from "coldest of winds" to "seaweed snarled" to "night's slow poison." Parading the images by at a stately but relentless pace, Kees uses what could be called a jump-cut to evoke the unalterable course of his imagination. The accumulation of details transforms the daughter from "the innocence of morning flesh" to "the cruel / Bride of a syphilitic or a fool."

Although conventional in its use of rhyme, and relaxed in its tone, the poem is unconventional in its challenge of the reader's notions of redemption and hope. It's the very quietness of the voice animating the poem that one finds so disturbing. Kees isn't trying to convince the reader that the world is bleak; he does nothing to hector us into agreeing with him. There are neither the bold, expansive declarations one finds in Ginsberg's "Howl" nor the self-lacerating, self-pitying disclosures one finds in Lowell's *Life Studies,* both of which Kees's first book of poetry preceded by more than a decade. Rather, by using a subject the reader is inclined to associate with the themes of transcendence and redemption, Kees inverts all expectations.

If Kees's poem suggests how cut off he was from both hope and others, O'Hara's early poem "Autobiographia Literaria" also evokes a vision of isolation. However, O'Hara's seclusion is neither as total nor as final as Kees's. For O'Hara, there is redemption in poetry itself, even if it is only temporary:

> When I was a child
> I played by myself in a
> corner of the schoolyard
> all alone.
>
> I hated dolls and I
> hated games, animals were
> not friendly and birds
> flew away.
>
> If anyone was looking
> for me I hid behind a
> tree and cried out "I am
> an orphan."
>
> And here I am, the
> center of all beauty!
> writing these poems!
> Imagine!

O'Hara has divided the poem into four unrhymed quatrains, with each of the first three consisting of one self-contained sentence. O'Hara uses the line breaks to break up the sinuous fluidity of each sentence, shifting it from one direction to another. Through his use of overstatement ("I hated dolls") and exaggeration ("birds / flew away"), O'Hara details a poignant, yet self-mocking vision of a lonely childhood.

O'Hara uses irony to confront a familiar stereotype of homosexuality, particularly in the 1950s: "I hated dolls." His dismissal calls into question our presumption of how a young boy is supposed to behave. If we expect young boys to hate dolls and other toys associated with being a girl, what does it mean when a male poet finds it necessary to make what should be an obvious statement? Like Kees, O'Hara expects no sympathy from the reader. Why should he when he is "the / center of all beauty! / writing these poems"?

Beyond their rejection of the reader's sympathy, the other affinity that O'Hara shares with Kees is his ability to invert the reader's expectations. By the poem's third stanza, O'Hara has set the stage for the poet as a child who played by himself in the corner of a schoolyard, and was ostracized by his schoolmates and by animals. The third stanza opens with someone looking for the poet, who, instead of welcoming human contact, hides behind a tree and cries out: "I am / an orphan." By exaggerating his feelings of isolation, O'Hara uses the surrealist technique of an extreme and disjunctive comparison to deflect any sympathy we might have for his isolation. Instead, he announces his total social isolation. The line break interrupts the poet's declaration, as well as reinforces the jolt we get when we realize the poet is making a statement of self-sufficiency. O'Hara is not only mocking himself; he is also mocking the reader.

The subverting tone sets both Kees's and O'Hara's poems apart from the work of many of their contemporaries; they are making fun of sentiment because they don't trust it, and because they know how easily it can devolve into the sentimental. In fact, Kees uses his awareness of the reader's desire for palatable sentiment to fuel "For My Daughter." He wants to compel his readers to reflect upon their expectations, and, in this regard, the poem functions like an accusing mirror.

II.

In the fall of 1949, Kees, who had written for *Time* and *Paramount Newsreel*, began writing art reviews for the *Nation*. He replaced Clement Greenberg, whom he would later make fun of in a limerick he included in a letter sent to a friend.[4] By this time, Kees numbered among his friends artists such as William Baziotes, Fritz Bultman, Hans Hofmann, and Robert Motherwell. His paintings and collages were beginning to be taken seriously. He eventually had four solo exhibitions at the Peridot Gallery, which also exhibited work by Louise Bourgeois, Hans Hofmann, and Bradley Walker Tomlin. For three consecutive summers (1947–49), he and his wife, Ann, stayed in Provincetown, where many artists and writers gathered, and where Hofmann taught. He wrote essays and poems for catalogs and brochures. After moving to California, he made friends with Hassel Smith and Edward Corbett, as well as resumed his friendship with Janet Richards, who had been married to Manny Farber, a film reviewer, critic, and painter.

O'Hara moved to New York in the fall of 1951, one year after Kees left New York for California. He got a job at the front desk of the Museum of Modern Art. After working as an editorial associate for *ARTnews* from 1953 to '55, he rejoined the staff at the museum as a special assistant in the International Program of the Museum of Modern Art. In 1960 he was made assistant curator of paintings and sculptures for the museum, and in 1965 he was promoted to associate curator. O'Hara wrote about art, curated important exhibitions, and collaborated with artists. He was the subject of paintings by Larry Rivers, Fairfield Porter, Elaine de Kooning, and Alice Neel, and he dedicated poems to Norman Bluhm, Grace Hartigan, and Joan Mitchell, among others. Shortly after his death, the Museum of Modern Art honored O'Hara's presence and memory.[5]

Kees and O'Hara were right where the action was, particularly when it came to the rise of the Abstract Expressionists, and artists such as Jackson Pollock and Willem de Kooning. Both men were active participants in the downtown New York art scene long before others knew that that world existed. In 1948, Kees wrote a review of an exhibition by Robert Motherwell. In 1965, in the exhibition catalog O'Hara wrote to accompany a retrospective exhibition of Motherwell's paintings and collages he had organized for the Museum of Modern Art, Kees's review is the earliest listed in the bibliography. Certainly, what Kees wrote about Motherwell in the March 1948 issue of *Magazine of Art* helped establish the parameters for O'Hara's catalog essay:

> His circular forms are not oranges or abstractions of oranges, heads or abstractions of heads; his rectangles, blots, blurs and brushstrokes assert nothing but their own existence, their own identity and individuality. They are objects from their own world, and that world is the world of paint. Motherwell's insistence upon this concentration and definition is as fierce as Celine's insistence on hell on earth or the insistence of the air on its own transparency.[6]

In light of his apparent suicide, Kees's linking of Motherwell's "circular forms" with "Celine's insistence of hell on earth" tells us more about the poet than the artist. But it should also be noted that he understands that paint can be paint, and thus is open to the idea of words being words.

About Motherwell's series of paintings *Elegy to the Spanish Republic,* O'Hara writes:

> And always there is an absolute belief in the reality of the schema, executed with such force that individual paintings of the series have been variously interpreted as male verticals and female ovoids, as bulls' tails and testicles hung side by side on the wall of the arena after the fight, and as purist formal juxtapositions of rectangular and curvilinear forms. As with the great recent painting *Africa,* the possibility of the schema's arousing such a broad range of associations, depending on the emotional vocabulary of the viewer, is a sign of its power to communicate in a truly abstract way, while never losing its identity as a pictorial statement.[7]

Whether O'Hara had Kees's review in mind when he wrote his essay is not the issue. Clearly, both poets were able to look at painting in a nonliterary way. They didn't need narrative or recognizable images to be convinced of its seriousness. That they both understood that in America in the late 1940s, beginning with the poured paintings of Jackson Pollock, painting could successfully shed all of these historical aspects and be about paint, is central to an understanding of their poetry. For while Kees and O'Hara were attracted to literary forms, villanelles and sestinas in Kees's case, and odes and elegies in O'Hara's, they also wrote poetry that was open and nonliterary. The difference is that O'Hara did so in a sustained and innovative way, and Kees did not.

Like other poets of their respective generations, Kees and O'Hara began their careers exploring various literary forms, but in sharp contrast to many of their peers, they became deeply engaged by modernist painting. Their involvement made them realize that the sources of poetry extended beyond literary tradition to include seemingly banal things and ordinary events of daily life. In their attempt to bring American speech into poetry, Kees and O'Hara not only implicitly acknowledged the influence of William Carlos Williams but also became interested in an open-ended poem.

Kees and O'Hara derived their subjects from popular culture, and from the world they inhabited. They wrote about an urban landscape that was defined as much by the media (cheap novels, movies, and art) as by its denizens. Kees's first book, *The Last Man,* for example, contains the poem "The Scene of the Crime," which derives its subject from the tabloids. Again in contrast to their contemporaries, Kees and O'Hara were to varying degrees able to shed the linear narrative governing a poem. On November 27, 1948, Kees wrote in a letter to Norris Getty: "Hofmann asked me to write a poem for the catalog of his Paris show."[8] "A Salvo for Hans Hofmann," the largely unrhymed poem that Kees wrote, marks a change in his approach to poetry. In contrast to the airtight argument of "For My Daughter," the images function in a less direct, more abstract way:

> Out of summer's heat, the winter's cold,
> The look of harbors and the trees,
>
> The shared world traced again and again,
> Enriched, enlarged, caught in a burning scrutiny
>
> Like fog-lamps on a rotten night. The scraps
> Of living shift and change. Because of you,
>
> The light burns sharper in how many rooms,
> Shaped to a new identity; the dark hall
>
> Finds a door; the wind comes in;
> A rainbow sleeps and wakes against the wall.

The opening juxtaposition of opposites ("summer's heat, the winter's cold") suggests that Kees was familiar with Surrealist poetry and art by the late 1940s. In a letter dated June 1943, Kees mentions that the recent issue of *View* magazine has "eight poems by e. e. cummings."[9] Edited by Charles Henri Ford and published in New York, *View* was a lively journal of the arts. In contrast to other little magazines of the period, the primary focus of *View,* both in literature and art, was Surrealism. It had covers by Joseph Cornell and Marcel Duchamp, and included reproductions of paintings by Andre Masson, Yves Tanguy, Max Ernst, Kurt Seligmann, Pavel Tchelitchev, and other Europeans who moved to America during the war.

The particular issue of *View* Kees mentions is number 2, from June 1943.[10] The cover was by the American artist Man Ray, and, in addition to cummings's contribution, it contained a translation of the essay "Magic: The Flesh and Blood of Poetry," by the French Surrealist poet Benjamin Peret; a review of Rainer Maria Rilke and Wallace Stevens by Harold Rosenberg, who later became an influential art critic and coined the term "action painting"; and the first publication of poems by the precocious American Surrealist poet Philip Lamantia.

Kees also published his poem "The Furies" in the *Tiger's Eye,* another little magazine that focused on literature and art. Like *View,* the *Tiger's Eye*'s editorial policy was favorably disposed to Surrealism and members of the Abstract Expressionist generation; it reproduced work by Louise Bourgeois and William Baziotes, among others, and was one of the first American magazines to publish the writings of Antonin Artaud.

Hans Hofmann, who had asked Kees to write "A Salvo," was a highly influential artist and teacher whose students included Larry Rivers, Paul Resika, Paul Georges, and Jane Freilicher. (River and Freilicher became close friends of Frank O'Hara.) In his poem, Kees has utilized his awareness of Hofmann's theory of push-pull to create a poem where the reader's attention is constantly being shifted from image to image, from "summer's heat" to "winter"s cold." Neither Hofmann's paintings nor this particular poem of Kees make an attempt at realism. Rather, it is "the look of harbors and the trees" that the artist traces; it is this "shared world" that he enlarges and enriches.

Throughout the poem, Kees evokes the different kinds of weather that he and Hofmann have experienced while living and working in Provincetown during the summer. It's out of this matrix that the poem is created. And yet, while the poem (and presumably also the painting) owes something to the natural world, it doesn't become a picturesque scene. Kees's discontinuous images don't add up to either an imagist postcard or a story. There are abrupt shifts in visual detail, which the poet underscores with line breaks, such as the one that takes place between "burning scrutiny" and "Like fog-lamps on a rotten night."

Kees's simile, "Like fog-lamps on a rotten night," serves a dual function; it returns our attention to "winter's cold, / The look of harbors and the trees," as well as inverts our expectation. There is something jarring in the parallel Kees establishes between the "shared world" and "burning scrutiny," and a "rotten night" examined by a "fog-lamp." The causal world is no longer central to painting or to writing. "The scraps / Of living shift and change. Because of you," Kees writes in the following lines, again raising the reader's expectations, as well as using a conditional statement to connect what precedes with what follows: "Because of you, / The light burns sharper in how many rooms." Kees believes the artist is able to both shape and synthesize the light of the world and of seeing (fog-lamp, burning scrutiny) into a "new identity." What the artist transforms, and what Kees parallels in the poem, is light. The poem moves from "summer's heat" to "winter's cold" to "burning scrutiny" to "fog-lamp" to light" to "a rainbow" which possesses animistic properties; it sleeps and wakes. The line is open-ended enough to suggest that it is also a painting.

Written a few months after Kees wrote his essay on Robert Motherwell, "A Salvo for Hans Hofmann" reveals how much he had absorbed from his friendship with various Abstract Expressionists. In contrast to his earlier poems, Kees has written a nonnarrative poem in which details are no longer paraded by, but instead are transformed from stanza to stanza, and from line to line. Kees's poem articulates a vision of constant metamorphosis. In its combination of disparate images, "A Salvo for Hans Hofmann" owes a debt to Surrealism. At the same time, echoing the Abstract Expressionists' interest in nonhierarchical, all-over composition, each image in Kees's poem is of equal importance. Because "A Salvo for Hans Hofmann" is one of the few poems Kees wrote in response to an Abstract Expressionist painting,[11] one wonders why the poet didn't write more poems in this vein. Certainly, he was in the thick of things. But like much else he did in his short life, the writing didn't satisfy some deep need in him. In this case, the subject (Hofmann's paintings) didn't allow him to register his pessimism.

Frank O'Hara wrote "Joseph Cornell" in 1955; it is shaped like two boxes, one above the other, in a deliberate allusion to Cornell's shadow boxes:

Into a sweeping meticulously-
detailed disaster the violet
light pours. It's not a sky,
it's a room. And in the open
field a glass of absinthe is
fluttering its song of India.
Prairie winds circle mosques.

You are always a little too
young to understand. He is
bored with his sense of the
past the artist. One of the
prescient rock in his heart
he has spread a land without
flowers of near distances.

The first "box" is O'Hara's verbal equivalent of a Cornell box. The light doesn't come from the sky (the outside, natural world) but from the room itself. The metaphysical world it evokes is both American and exotic: "Prairie winds circle mosques." In contrast to Kees's "A Salvo for Hans Hofmann," O'Hara's lines are more self-sufficient, more surprising. At the same time, like Kees, O'Hara constantly shifts the focus, like someone moving between a telescope and a magnifying glass: "It's not a sky, / it's a room. And in the open / field a glass of absinthe is / fluttering its song of India." This shifting of perspective is O'Hara's equivalent of Cornell's boxes, which not only articulated an entire world, but also often contained astronomical maps and other references to a world that exists on the edge of the visible.

In the second box, O'Hara abruptly changes the focus from the box to the viewer. We, it seems, are "always a little too / young to understand" that an artist gets bored with the past, and must create new forms. O'Hara's emphasis on the new brings to mind Kees's "new identity." Whereas O'Hara believed the artist possesses the power to create new forms out of a barren world ("a land without / flowers of near distances"), Kees didn't always believe one could transform the barrenness (or what Eliot called the "Waste Land") into art. For him, the world was bleak and irredeemable. In this regard, "A Salvo for Hans Hofmann" is one of the exceptions in Kees's deeply pessimistic oeuvre. And while the rainbow can be understood as a covenant made between the artist and nature, it also seems like a symbol; it can be read as a literary intrusion in an otherwise nonliterary poem or as a description of a painting. O'Hara had more faith in the transformative power of love and in art. As in his earlier poem, "Autobiographia Literaria," O'Hara believes that art makes redemption possible, and that in making art or writing poetry the individual finds temporary solace.

III.

Kees's voice is quiet and intimate; he is full of despair but he refuses to complain. Rather, he makes chilling observations: "Sleep is too short a death."[12] For him, the movies provide an ironic contrast to life; they represent an unattainable fairy-tale world. Thus, in one of his late poems, "1926," Kees writes:

> The porchlight coming on again,
> Early November, the dead leaves
> Raked in piles, the wicker swing
> Creaking. Across the lots
> A phonograph is playing *Ja-Da.*
>
> An orange moon. I see the lives
> Of neighbors, mapped and marred
> Like all the wars ahead, and R.
> Insane, B. with his throat cut,
> Fifteen years from now, in Omaha.
>
> I didn't know them then.
> My airedale scratches at the door.
> And I am back from seeing Milton Sills
> And Doris Kenyon. Twelve years old.
> The porchlight coming on again.

The poem collapses present and past, knowledge and innocence. Memory, like the cycle of time the poem evokes (seasons, night, and moon), is inescapable; it can displace the individual, make him feel intensely isolated. In "1926," the past rises to the surface of the poet's consciousness in the form of distinct images. Out of these images emerges a memory; the poet is twelve and coming home from a movie starring "Milton Sills / And Doris Kenyon."

Kees tells nothing more about either the film or the stars; he presumes that the reader knows who they are. And yet Sills and Kenyon are figures from the world of Hollywood, not ones found in literature or myth. They were well-known silent film stars who were married and who often starred together in adventure romances. In this regard, they are emblematic of the ideal in which art and life are synonymous. But, while they were famous in their time, Sills and Kenyon are barely remembered now. However, to a twelve-year-old on the brink of puberty, this dashing young couple is as powerful as the gods, which is the point Kees makes. And these gods, like all the others Kees alludes to in his poems, ultimately fail to deliver what they promise. For Kees, art and life never merge and become one.

Beginning with "The porchlight coming on again," Kees describes a scene in which someone (we later learn it is a twelve-year-old boy) sees and hears rather banal aspects of the world around him with a heightened consciousness. In their cinematic self-sufficiency, the images evoke the loneliness and vulnerability of someone walking through a deserted neighborhood at night; everything is ominous. The poet isn't remembering the past so much as being invaded by it. The poem registers the present tense of memory.

The poem moves swiftly from image to image, like a movie camera. Porchlight, leaves, wicker swing—everything is either changing, still, or moving. The world is in flux, which suggests that any sense of order one might have is not to be trusted. The discontinuous, cinematic fragments are simultaneously complete and incomplete. The steady tumble of images parallels the poet's consciousness; the memories are surfacing one after another, and he is unable to stop and contemplate them. At no point does his attention linger; he is, after all, walking home late at night. It should be noted here that Kees's discontinuities and shifting angles of perspective anticipate O'Hara, particularly in poems such as "On the Way to the San Remo," which begins:

> The black ghinkos snarl their way up
> the moon growls at each blinking window
> the apartment houses climb deafeningly into the purple

O'Hara, however, is more exuberant and wild than Kees in his use of verbs. One could say that Kees, who worked on newsreels, is employing a documentary visual style, while O'Hara is using a disorienting, animating style.

The poet (and the reader) see the porchlight coming on, see a raked pile of dead leaves, hear (and see) the wicker swing, hear the phonograph; an atmosphere of order and loneliness permeates Kees's few telling images. Without leaving the present, we (the poet and the reader) are thrust into the past. Within this context, the "porchlight" becomes a sign of safety and security; it is his home and we suspect it is not enough. From the porchlight that opens the poem literally and figuratively, the poet shifts in the second stanza to "an orange moon," and then just as abruptly Kees declares, "I see the lives / Of neighbors, mapped and marred. . . ." His neighbors are doomed to suffer awful fates: one dies insane, the other has his throat cut or has cut his own throat. There is no escape; the future is fatal.

Kees is returning to a subject he explored in "For My Daughter," which is about a parent's inability to protect his child from the future and mortality. Only this time, one might say that he is the unprotected child. The third stanza begins: "I didn't know them then." It is only later, after disasters have befallen all his neighbors, whom Kees never mentions by name, that he learns something about them. He also recognizes in their fate something about himself and his future.

In his use of discontinuous, self-contained images, and in his repetition of the first line as the last line, Kees has absorbed lessons not only from cinema, but also from the Abstract Expressionists, particularly their use of shifting and/or multiple perspectives. The poem doesn't unfold according to linear time. Rather, Kees has collapsed present and past together, in effect creating a time warp where the past keeps repeating itself in the present, and the "porchlight" comes on again and again; and each time it does so, it offers less and less hope because, in real time, he is further and further away from that moment.

If the typical autobiographical poem of the 1950s utilizes a circular structure of present–past–return to the present with renewed insight, as Marjorie Perloff suggests,[13] Kees reveals no affinity for this structure in the 1940s, nearly a decade before O'Hara wrote his first memorable poems. In "1926," the "I" only now understands something about this past world, particularly his neighbors, which it didn't before: "I didn't know them then." The present "I" sees beyond the surfaces the past "I" saw, and which are now surfacing in the poet's consciousness. And yet, it is the past ("the porchlight") that dominates. Memory and pessimism haunt Kees and he seems unable to find his way out of the labyrinth they construct around him.

The "I" in Kees's poem observes fragments of the world in the first stanza. In the second stanza, the observation goes from the outside world of dead leaves and the moon to the interiors of the houses lining his neighborhood ("I see the lives / Of neighbors, mapped and marred"). But this observation is made by Kees the poet, and not the adolescent boy in the poem walking home one night after the movies. The adolescent boy is still enthralled by the surface of movies, by images, while the adult "I" is painfully aware of the raw substance of people's lives. The "I" of the poem is fragmented; it lives in different time periods, past and present, without being able to reconcile them.

The third stanza brings us back to the past, where the adolescent boy has finished walking home: "My airedale scratches at the door. / And I am back from seeing Milton Sills / And Doris Kenyon. Twelve years old." But this memory of innocence is now thoroughly tainted by what Kees has learned about his neighbors in the intervening years. He draws no sustenance from it, no joy. The porchlight that illuminated his home, like a lighthouse beacon, has become remote, more so now that the poet is remembering it. He will in effect never be able to reach it; he will only be able to see it coming on again and again. And with that memory comes the knowledge of what happened to his neighbors.

As both the first and the last line in the poem, "The porchlight coming on again" underscores the impossibility of reaching sanctuary; becoming an adult means to be exiled from home. Kees's memories reify a feeling, which is part of his consciousness. Suffusing the poem is an air of cosmic fatalism, which is suggested most intensely in the phrase "mapped and marred." His neighbors' futures and by implication his own are doomed from the start. The terse precision of Kees's language recalls the clipped sentences of Raymond Chandler, whose novels he liked very much.[14] A short-story writer before he became a poet, Kees had a novelist's eye for telling details.

While Kees's use of a fragmented, observant "I," his reference to minor Hollywood stars, and the cinematic vérité of his images can be said to have prefigured O'Hara's poetry, one must also take into account the impact the Abstract Expressionists had on both these poets. Both Kees and O'Hara were members of a milieu in which artists were feverishly reassessing subject matter. They were early, sympathetic witnesses who on their own had embraced popular culture, particularly as it was manifested in the movies and in jazz. They were iconoclasts who thought the notion of high culture was suspect.

In terms of historical events, the difference is that Kees was part of this art scene near its beginning, when artists were starting to strip away narrative, the picturesque, and subject matter. He participated in their move toward abstraction, but he didn't ever get comfortably beyond the literary. O'Hara entered the scene a few years later, when the art scene had changed. Modern art was still frowned upon by many, but its advocates now included such institutions as the prestigious Museum of Modern Art, where O'Hara would work as a curator. He was sympathetic not only to older artists, such as de Kooning and Franz Kline, but also to younger artists, such as Larry Rivers and Jane Freilicher, both of whom worked in a figurative mode, and to Jasper Johns and Robert Rauschenberg, who were seen as both neo-dadaists and the originators of Pop art.

The other difference is that O'Hara is far more radical in his writing than Kees. Early on, O'Hara found inspiration in Whitman, whereas Kees seems to have come to him rather late in his short career, particularly in his long (for him) poem "Travels in North America," which was written after Kees and his wife, Ann, drove from New York City to California in the fall of 1950. However, Kees never wrote anything as long or as wild as O'Hara's "Second Avenue," which was written in 1953.[15] Kees's catalog of places and people does not have the same range as one finds in even the most documentary passages of "Second Avenue":

From "Travels in North America"

And sometimes, shivering in St. Paul or baking in Atlanta
The sudden sense that you have seen it all before:
The man who took your ticket at the Gen in Council Bluffs
Performed a similar function for you at the Shreveport Tivoli.
Joe's Lunch appears again, town after town, next door
To Larry's Shoe Repair, adjoining, inescapably, the Acme
Doughnut shop.

There is joylessness in Kees's weary poem. No matter where he is, he sees sameness. If one contrasts Kees's list with O'Hara's "Second Avenue," the difference in their temperaments is immediately apparent:

Now in November, by Josephine Johnson. The Heroes
by John Ashbery. Topper's Roumanian Broilings. The
Swimmer.
Your feet are more beautiful than your father's, I think,
does that upset you? I admire youth above age, yes,
in the infancy of the race when we were very upset we wrote,
"O toe!" and it took months to get those feet. Render. Rent.
Now more features of our day become popular, the nose
broken, the head bald, the body beautiful. Marilyn Monroe.

Kees doesn't interrupt himself or exploit the humor latent in such lines as "Joe's Lunch appears again." O'Hara is self-mocking and excited, and he often exploits the puns and associations certain words evoke by their very pronunciation. Thus, "Render" is followed by "Rent." But these differences are not the deepest and most telling ones separating Kees and O'Hara; they point to them.

Where Kees addresses his poem to one person, the reader, in a quiet unveering voice, O'Hara often employs a combination of voices that veer from intimate and gossipy to public and parodic. In "Ave Maria," he begins with an imperative:

Mothers of America
let your kids go to the movies!

The opening line is a perfectly pitched parody of the fearful, fear-inducing voice of official authority. "Mothers of America," the poem begins, and one expects some dire warning will follow. But the warning the poem delivers, "let your kids go to the movies!" is subversive on two levels; it mocks the official voice, as well as suggests that mothers should be more indulgent with their children. There is a playful generosity animating O'Hara's language that you will never encounter in Kees's poetry. O'Hara's poem is a run-on sentence, a manic, mocking monologue in which a lot of serious observations are made.

For O'Hara, the movies are good for the soul; they are the light guiding the inner life ("but what about the soul / that grows in darkness, embossed by silvery images"). The movies allow the adult to enter "some glamorous country / they first saw on a Saturday afternoon or playing hookey. . . ." The movies may have offered Kees (as an adolescent) a vision of romance and adventure, but they didn't help him find his way out of a darkness that proved suicidal. The "glamorous country" didn't offset "the dead leaves / Raked in piles." Even the memory of the porchlight of his childhood home offers no consolation. This is what finally and most deeply separates Kees from O'Hara. Kees's adolescent walks home from the movies alone at night, isolated from everyone, while O'Hara's adolescents may get lucky at the movies, where they are playing hookey, and have "their first sexual experience . . . with a pleasant stranger." At the beginning of his career, O'Hara could cry out, "I am / an orphan," whereas near the end of his life Kees was convinced that he had been orphaned by the world. For him, ordinary sleep wasn't long enough, so he sought and most likely found another.

NOTES

1. O'Hara didn't fulfill the stereotype of the poet as an isolated, angst-ridden, suffering individual (Robert Lowell, John Berryman, Karl Shapiro) who relied on irony and metrics to make his alienation known. His references were not solely literary, or, if they were literary, they alluded to modernist poets, such as Pierre Reverdy and Vladimir Mayakovsky, who were not canonized in America. There was a casual tone to his work which readers took literally, failing to see his technical innovations. In addition, O'Hara lived in New York, didn't teach, and

wrote about art, all of which he made clear in his poems. Consisting largely of artists and young poets, the first audience for O'Hara—and for John Ashbery, James Schuyler, Barbara Guest, and Kenneth Koch, all members of the so-called New York School—was seen as a coterie, which the mainstream literary world was quick to dismiss as irrelevant. That O'Hara and others have been accepted by the mainstream literary world doesn't mean that it has opened their doors to radical practitioners.

2. *Furioso* 4 (Winter 1949), a little magazine published in Minnesota, contained poems by John Ashbery and Weldon Kees.

3. Robert E. Knoll, ed., *Weldon Kees and the Midcentury Generation: Letters, 1935–1955* (Lincoln: University of Nebraska Press, 1986), p. 125; Edward Lucie-Smith, "An Interview with Frank O'Hara," in *Standing Still and Walking in New York,* ed. Donald Allen (1975; rpt., San Francisco: Grey Fox, 1983), pp. 3–26 (note: the interview was conducted in Oct. 1965).

4.

An erstwhile "whole surface" man, Clem
Plucked himself off at the stem,
And sent out the word
To the avant-garde herd:
  "All-over: is over;
  It's finished; moreover,
  DeKooning does not
  In a word, 'hit the spot.'"
And that's the new gospel, pro tem.

Written in Dec. 1951, the limerick appears in Knoll, *Weldon Kees,* pp. 162–63. Kees is poking fun at Greenberg, who had once championed "all-over" painting, but was now predicting that important painting would no longer be "all-over" but "focal," or have a center of attention. It is clear from the limerick that Kees did not align himself with the influential formalist criticism of Greenberg.

5. Published after his death, *In Memory of My Feelings, A Selection of Poems by Frank O'Hara,* ed. Bill Berkson (New York: Museum of Modern Art, 1967), contained "original decorations" by thirty artists, a preface by Rene d'Harnoncourt, and an afterword by Bill Berkson. Among the artists contributing work were Norman Bluhm, Willem de Kooning, Jane Freilicher, Grace Hartigan, Jasper Johns, Alex Katz, Alfred Leslie, and Larry Rivers.

6. Knoll, *Weldon Kees,* p. 109.

7. *Robert Motherwell* (New York: Museum of Modern Art, 1965), p. 19.

8. Knoll, *Weldon Kees,* p. 117. The reference is to Hans Hofmann (1880–1966), an influential teacher and painter whom Kees met in Provincetown.

9. Knoll, *Weldon Kees,* p. 82.

10. Charles Henri Ford, ed., comp. Catrina Nieman and Paul Nathan, foreword by Paul Bowles, introduction by Catrina Neiman, *View: Parade of the Avant-Garde 1940–1947* (New York: Thunder's Mouth Press, 1991), pp. 274–75 (see "Index to *View:* 1940–1947," comp. Judith Young Malin, pp. 271–82).

11. Kees dedicated his poem "Turtle" to his friend William Baziotes. See Weldon Kees, *Collected Poems,* p. 101.

12. Knoll, *Weldon Kees,* p. 64.

13. "Sometime when you're in need of a good escape reading you might look into the works of an author who has been pleasing Ann and me very much indeed. The name is Raymond Chandler; he writes very marvelous mystery stories and does the best job of dissecting Southern California of anyone I've yet encountered." From a letter to Norris Getty, May 2, 1942.

14. Knoll, *Weldon Kees,* p. 64.

15. Perloff, *Frank O'Hara,* p. 69.

The Poet as Art Critic

> The coordinates of this position might be ill defined, its fragility or strength unassessed, its motivations unconscious; still the position stands, and stands *for* and *against.*
>
> —Yve-Alain Bois, *Painting as Model*

The publication of John Ashbery's *Selected Prose,* edited by Eugene Richie (2004), offers us the opportunity to begin considering what he has, in his position as an art critic, stood for and against. And once we have done so, this may enable us to begin teasing out the relationship between his art criticism and his poetry, how they might have influenced each other. It may also allow consideration of the position taken by Frank O'Hara (1926–66), Ashbery's contemporary and close friend, in his art writing. Ashbery and O'Hara are the only two poets of the original five associated with the New York School to have made a living from working in the art world. Both James Schuyler and Barbara Guest wrote reviews and essays, but neither of them ever supported themselves as art critics. The fifth poet, Kenneth Koch, taught at Columbia and was never an art critic.

Selected Prose brings together what the author calls "miscellaneous prose pieces written over the last half century." It augments *Reported Sightings: Art Chronicles, 1957–1987,* edited by David Bergman (1989), which includes over one hundred articles and reviews, most of which Ashbery wrote during the years he worked for *ARTnews, Art in America, Newsweek,* and *New York.* The sixty-nine pieces in *Selected Prose* include reviews of poetry and fiction; art criticism; essays on artists who wrote (and vice versa); five essays of varying length on Raymond Roussel (the

From *American Poetry Review,* vol. 34, no. 3 (May–June 2005).

most on one figure); prefaces and introductions to books; introductions to poetry readings; public lectures; reminiscences; essays on film, music, photography, and architecture; and an obituary. They appeared in *Poetry, Portfolio and ARTnews Annual, Book Week,* the *New York Times Book Review, ARTnews, PN Review, Edge,* the *Poetry Project Newsletter,* and *Modern Painters.* While *Selected Prose* and *Reported Sightings* add up to more than seven hundred pages, the two books represent just a fraction of Ashbery's total activities as an art critic and literary essayist. Based on the six Charles Eliot Norton lectures that he gave at Harvard University in 1989–90, *Other Traditions* (2000) is around 150 pages long, and includes essays on John Clare, Thomas Lovell Beddoes, Raymond Roussel, John Wheelwright, Laura Riding, and David Schubert, writers who, at best, barely have a toehold in the canon. Ashbery could have played it safe in the talks and spoken about canonical figures, but he didn't.

According to his bibliographer, David Kermani, Ashbery published over 450 articles, reviews, and essays about art between 1957 and 1975. This does not include his contributions to art catalogs and book reviews and other kinds of writing and writing work he did during this period; his stints as the critic for *New York* (1978–80) and *Newsweek* (1980–85); or catalog essays and introductions he has written since 1975. As Ashbery readily admits: "Some were written for money to help subsidize my poetry habit." But it is also true that many were written because he was commissioned to write about a subject he "was interested in." It should go without saying that this position is the one every art critic tries to occupy and maintain. Otherwise, writing becomes sheer drudgery.

O'Hara's criticism and related writing are collected in three books totaling around 375 pages: *Art Chronicles 1954–1966* (1975), *Standing Still and Walking in New York,* edited by Donald Allen (1975), and *What's With Modern Art,* with an afterword by Bill Berkson (1999). After graduating from Harvard, where he, Ashbery, and Kenneth Koch met, and receiving an M.A. from the University of Michigan, O'Hara moved to New York, and worked in the art world from 1952 to 1966. A charismatic figure, he soon became a highly visible, active force in the burgeoning art scene, a dervish toward whom different groups, factions, and individuals gravitated. As Philip Guston said after O'Hara died, "he was our Apollinaire."

Ashbery, who has stated that he "backed into a career as an art critic," began writing art reviews in 1957, though not on a regular basis. In 1960, while living in Paris, he became the art critic for the *New York Herald Tribune* (international edition) and continued in this position until 1965, when he returned to New York and became an executive editor at *ARTnews,* a position he held until 1972. In 1974, after being unemployed for more than a year, he began teaching creative writing at Brooklyn College (1974–90). While teaching at Brooklyn College, he was the art critic for *New York* (1978–80) and *Newsweek* (1980–85), which means that after he had received three major literary awards—the National Book Award, the Pulitzer Prize, and the National Book Critics Circle Award—for *Self-Portrait in a Convex Mirror* (1975), he still found it necessary to work at two full-time jobs.

While Ashbery and O'Hara operated in the art world, they functioned as mirror opposites. Ashbery lived and worked in Paris, far from New York, which had overtaken Paris and become the center of the international art world. He was the art critic for a newspaper and a magazine, which is one step removed from the action. O'Hara lived in New York and, at the time of his death, was associate curator of painting and sculpture at the Museum of Modern Art. Amid the rise of Pop art and Minimalism, as well as pronouncements of the death of painting, the failure of the so-called second generation, and the increasing number of art historians writing criticism, he was a magnet at the center of a storm.

Being an art critic is for the most part a low-paying job. It is particularly insecure if you do not have a position at a university. In the 1950s and '60s, it was far worse than it is now. In an informative interview with the English poet and literary critic Mark Ford, Ashbery talked about the financial side of being an art critic living in Paris:

> I got the job of art critic for the *Herald Tribune,* but that wasn't until May 1960. That didn't pay anything but it did open the way to other things that did pay. Even after five years in the

> job I was only making about $30 an article, but they could pay slave wages because there were so many Americans in Paris who were dying for that kind of work. So I really just lived from hand to mouth.[1]

In 1961, in addition to his regular job at the *Herald Tribune,* Ashbery became the art critic for *Art International,* a magazine. He also wrote articles for *ARTnews.*

Ashbery may have felt that he had backed into his career as an art critic, but his first reviews are not tentative. In his first published review (on Bradley Walker Tomlin),[2] he is poetic and precise, and gets the viewer to want to look again:

> In *Number 8,* 1949, the nervous energy of a pattern which seems to be made up of scythes and swear-words in Chinese is tempered by the sweet blue background. This contrast between form and color was to be the central idea in all the pictures Tomlin painted until his death in 1953.[3]

Often, after offering a close reading of the subject he is reviewing, he steps back and argues eloquently for both the difficult and the impossible. He ends his review of Gertrude Stein's *Stanzas in Meditation* (1956) for *Poetry Magazine* with the following observation:

> *Stanzas in Meditation* is no doubt the most successful of her attempts to do what can't be done, to create a counterfeit reality more real than reality. And if, on laying the book aside, we feel that it is still impossible to accomplish the impossible, we are also left with the conviction that it is the only thing worth trying to do.[4]

Is it all that surprising that this was the first and last time Ashbery reviewed a book for *Poetry*? Shortly after publishing *Turandot and Other Poems* (1953) and *Some Trees* (1956), he started his career as a critic by defining a worthy aesthetic goal as doing "what can't be done," which is "to create a counterfeit reality more real than reality."

Three years later, in an essay on Pierre Reverdy, Ashbery wrote:

> The lines drift across the page as overheard human speech drifts across our hearing: fragments of conversation, dismembered advertising slogans or warning signs in the Metro appear and remain the rock crystal of the poem. And far from banishing poetry to the unconscious, he lets it move freely in and out of the conscious and unconscious. Since we do not inhabit either world exclusively, the result is moving and lifelike.[5]

Elsewhere in this review, while comparing Reverdy to the film director Robert Bresson, who "created an ascetically transparent world,"[6] Ashbery wrote:

> Like Reverdy he has a keen ear for *le langage de la tribu* and a deep feeling for nature. Trees, clouds, lakes, automobiles, the texture of a woman's skin and of her dress are shown for what they are and are also undetachable from the story being told; they are like electrodes in the limpid bath of a precise context.[7]

Already masterful in his ability to shift tones and focus, Ashbery has consciously rejected transparency, received notions of realism in poetry, and confession, all of which were (and still are) believed to be allegorical narratives that naturally culminate in revelation, universal truth, or epiphany. All too often, these states of illuminated insight are familiar and border on cliché. The revelation is not something the poet discovers in the process of writing, but is something he or she already possesses, and must figure out how to package. Such poems are full of detachable symbols and images, triggers that set off the reader's sympathetic Pavlovian response. Ashbery is against both the predictable and the detachable, which allow a poem to be reduced to a theme or to be summed up.

Ashbery's interest in both "counterfeit reality" and the "lifelike" helps explain why, nearly twenty years after writing about Stein and Reverdy, he would write his widely acclaimed poem "Self-Portrait in a Convex Mirror." The poem is ostensibly about Parmigianino's trompe l'oeil painting, a counterfeit reality that depicts the artist as if he is looking into a convex mirror. By being a "mirror" of the absent painter, the self-portrait displaces the viewer, who is standing where the artist once stood. We see his imprisoned reflection looking back us. On both the visceral level and in a larger sense, the artist's absence reminds us of our immediate and impending departure. At the same time, the painter stares at us, locked inside the wooden sphere, his hand in the foreground, as if protecting him from us and from time. This is one of the ways Ashbery describes the portrait:

> The soul has to stay where it is,
> Even though restless, hearing raindrops at the pane,
> The sighing of autumn leaves thrashed by the wind,
> Longing to be free, outside, but it must stay
> Posing in this place.

Don't poetry and art share the paradox of embodying a frozen time, while outside its domain time ("autumn leaves") keeps surging ahead?

Ashbery's description of Elizabeth Bishop's poetry is particularly apt about both his own writing and Parmigianino's arresting and disturbing painting:

> We live in a quandary, but it is not a dualistic conflict between inner and outer reality; it is rather a question of deciding how much the outer reality is our reality, how far we can advance into it and still keep a toe-hold on the inner, private one.[8]

Ashbery's observation also applies to his choices as an art critic. For one thing, he has never been known as a critic who either celebrated hyperbolically or grumbled mightily about the work of artists who were or weren't in the spotlight. I suspect this is because early on in his career he recognized that the outer reality (or what the art world is intently focusing on at a particular moment) would subsume him if he advanced too far into it. After all, he chose to live in Paris, not New York. And he never tried to stay young and become the Paul McCartney of art criticism.

Under the constant pressure of assignments, deadlines, and, for many years, low wages, Ashbery had to repeatedly negotiate and, out of necessity, define a position. For even in the journalistic world of weekly articles and monthly essays, one cannot remain a passive observer. As Yve-Alain Bois makes clear in his brilliant introduction to *Painting as Model,* "Any critical discourse is programmatic in part." However, when it comes to the criticism of Ashbery and O'Hara, neither the art world nor the literary establishment, mainstream or otherwise, has made any serious attempts to assess their accomplishments, and the positions they have taken. And when they have, both realms have tended to be dismissive. One of the few exceptions is Helen Vendler, whose essay on Ashbery's art criticism is full of astute observations and insights.[9] The other is Marjorie Perloff.[10]

In the 1950s, when Ashbery and O'Hara first began publishing in *ARTnews,* it was assumed that, in working for this magazine, one was writing for a general readership. At the same time, both men entered the art world just as it was beginning to morph wildly, until, like the Incredible Hulk, it became a lurching, contentious, muscle-bound version of its earlier self, with each muscle-bound version spawning yet another more extreme version. The art world was becoming a place for specialists armed with degrees, and writing for a general reader, even if this figure were a fiction, was regarded as frivolous. Among the many developments that had a considerable influence in the art world during the 1960s, one must mention the magazine *Artforum,* which was started in San Francisco in 1962 and moved to New York in 1967. There are four figures who had much to do with its rise to prominence as an influential review based in New York: Philip Leider, the founding editor; the art historians Michael Fried and Rosalind Krauss; and the film historian and theorist Annette Michelson.[11] In 1974, for reasons too complicated to go into here, Krauss and Michelson left *Artforum* and shortly afterward started *October.* Throughout the 1960s, the writing that appeared in *ARTnews* and *Art and America* was very different from the kind that appeared in the pages of *Artforum.*

This is how the art historian and theorist Hal Foster describes the opposition between the poet-critics associated with *ARTnews* and the art historians associated with *Artforum:*

> Yet for the critics who most marked *Artforum*—first Fried and [Barbara] Rose, then Michelson and Krauss—[Harold] Rosenberg was all "fustian writing," an aspersion that they

> also cast at poet-critics like Frank O'Hara and John Ashbery (and later Peter Schjeldahl and Carter Ratcliff) associated with *ARTnews* under its editor Tom Hess. This was not art criticism as "serious discipline."[12]

By "serious discipline," Foster means that none of the poets were either trained in art history or aligned with the formalist critic Clement Greenberg. Essentially, this means that none of them had developed a paradigm that they could apply to different works of art. The assumption is that the poet-critics didn't take positions or, if they did, they weren't worth serious consideration because they weren't rooted in a discourse accepted by academia. Foster believes poets are ruled by their mushy sensibilities. Clearly, the art world in which Ashbery and O'Hara were working during the '60s was a bubbling cauldron, with everything constantly being pushed to the boiling point.

Foster goes on to elaborate upon his understanding of the opposition:

> Of course such oppositions as formalist versus social-historical methods, and objective versus belle-lettristic styles, long preceded *Artforum,* but for this generation they were compounded most volatilely in its milieu. It was not an even match. Whereas the poet-critics had only an attenuated connection to the belle-lettristic reviews of the French Salons to stand on, the formalist followers of Greenberg could draw on the immediate prestige not only of New Criticism in literary studies but also of German art history as established in the American university by such prewar émigrés as Erwin Panofsky. The formalist camp felt that it had a near-scientific view of art history to support its semi-subjective judgments of aesthetic quality (here Fried aligns Greenberg with T. S. Eliot, and Leider relates his *Artforum* to *Scrutiny* under F. R. Leavis). No wonder such criticism appeared so powerful and, to its opponents, so presumptuous. "They were successfully putting over the impression," Ratcliff complains, "that they were writing the final draft of history as it happened."[13]

Three points in Foster's retelling merit further discussion. One is the notion that by aligning themselves with T. S. Eliot and New Criticism, the art historians could claim that they were mainstream intellectuals and thus central. It was they, not the poet-critics, who carried the torch of the "objective correlative" from the literary world to the art world. This view ignores the possibility that the poet-critics associated with *ARTnews* rejected New Criticism, which, after all, was being used to promote poets and poetry with which they had little affinity. Unlike many of their contemporaries, Ashbery and O'Hara did not become followers of Eliot or Ezra Pound. Clearly, the poetry world was already fractured, with Fried on one side and Ashbery and O'Hara on the other. The second point is that Foster doesn't recognize that American poet-critics didn't need to connect themselves to the belle-lettrist reviews of the French salons, because there was already an American belle-lettrist tradition. It included Parker Tyler, James Agee, and Manny Farber writing movie reviews,[14] Weldon Kees and Fairfield Porter writing art reviews, Virgil Thompson writing music reviews, and Edwin Denby writing dance reviews for various publications. The third point is the more serious charge that the poet-critics were not capable of "serious discipline," and that their writing was "fustian." The implication is that the poet-critics were some kind of sensitive plant, their heads easily turned.

Given the few examples that I have already cited of Ashbery's lifelong preoccupation with "counterfeit reality," the "lifelike," and living in a "quandary"—and I can assure the reader that there are many more such examples—I would argue that there is a remarkable consistency to his approach to art and literature. Ashbery's writing is crystalline, while O'Hara's is simultaneously hyperbolic and self-mocking. Neither is "fustian." I would further add that neither Ashbery nor O'Hara feels compelled to proclaim his seriousness; they don't feel compelled to justify themselves. Their criticism isn't theory driven, but object driven. Neither is prone to making generalizations, and both pay close attention to what is in front of them, which is not all that easy or simple to do.

Although not necessarily broadcast from the rooftops, a negative view of poet-critics still predominates in many quarters of the art world. And there are many reasons why the work of poet-critics is also largely ignored in the literary world. First of all, poet-critics like Ashbery and O'Hara wrote about art, rather than about poetry or themselves. Both the literary and the art worlds have become increasingly splintered and specialized, a contested and in many ways discontinuous field in which there is little consensus among the various factions, and very little overlap between them. The poet-critic exists in two worlds that for the most part don't even bother to recognize each other. At the same time, in each domain there are multiple manifestations of the opposition between those whose practice is defined as "serious discipline" and those who are said to rely on sensibility and something as vague and poetic as the muse. And let's not forget that there are those who believe that if you are a poet engaged in any kind of writing for a general audience, particularly if you make money from it, you must have compromised your higher self, and tainted forever both your soul and your capacity for serious poetry. Not only is integrity impossible in such a situation, but no wisdom is to be gained from constantly being in, and negotiating with, the world. According to this view, the only way a poet should exist is as a sequestered being who protects and cultivates his or her sensitivity.[15] Thus, Ashbery and O'Hara did exactly the opposite of what many other poets of their generation did. Instead of retreating from the world and living in the cloistered environment of universities, they entered into a situation that was gaining increasing attention from the public. And in terms of the public, the gap between the art world and the poetry world has only widened since the '60s. Warhol is a household name; O'Hara is not.

Foster's dismissive tone toward poet-critics, and his assertion elsewhere that they lack a paradigm,[16] reveals a lot about the hostilities they have to face. This may be one of the reasons why the poet-critic Raphael Rubinstein felt it was necessary to establish a distance between his writing and that of other poet-critics:

> Like so many other art critics, I am also a poet. I don't believe, however, that writing poetry is any particular qualification for writing about art. In fact, I generally don't like the art criticism of poets, even poets whose work I greatly admire. Frank O'Hara, for instance, is not to me an interesting art critic, though his poetry has taught me as much about art and artists as the work of any single critic.[17]

Whether this constitutes critique or narcissism, Rubinstein's conflicted evaluation of O'Hara's complex position is not an isolated example. In his article "Frank Appraisal," about the traveling exhibition "In Memory of My Feelings: Frank O'Hara and American Art" (organized by Russell Ferguson for the Museum of Contemporary Art, Los Angeles), Hilton Als also reveals that he is conflicted about O'Hara. There is the positive view:

> O'Hara believed that his role as a curator was not only to present the artist's view, but to enhance it with a view of his own (and recipients of such curatorial largesse included Jackson Pollock, Arshile Gorky, Franz Kline, and David Smith). He wasn't a trained art historian, which is why his work at MoMA was so refreshing and has never been duplicated: Innocence and joy cannot be duplicated.

Here are just two of Als's negative views:

> The voice of this particular poet: It is overestimated by mediocre graduate students and memoirists, who champion it and, like O'Hara, lack the discipline to write about things other than themselves.

And:

> He was the paradigm of the art-world fag that may make you avoid the art world now, and forever.[18]

While Frank O'Hara, who was not an artist, was the subject of a traveling museum exhibition (how often does this happen?), his name has largely been effaced at the Museum of Modern Art, where he worked for over a decade. At the time of his death, O'Hara had begun working on a retrospective of Jackson Pollock for the museum. The directorship of the exhibition was taken over by William S. Lieberman. Among the people who contributed research to the exhibition and accompanying exhibition catalog was the poet-critic William Berkson.[19] A little more than twenty years later, in 1998, the Museum of Modern Art hosted "Jackson Pollock." Kirk Varnedoe, chief curator of painting and sculpture at the museum, organized the exhibition, with assistance from Pepe Karmel, adjunct assistant curator in the museum's Department of Painting and Sculpture. A catalog of nearly 350 pages accompanied the exhibition.

In Varnedoe's heavily researched essay on Pollock, O'Hara isn't cited once in the more than two hundred footnotes. It's as if he were never at the museum and didn't write anything about Pollock, even something that Varnedoe disagreed with, or found distasteful. Given that O'Hara was working on Pollock's first retrospective for the museum at the time of his death, that he wrote the first monograph on the artist, *Jackson Pollock* (1959), and that he championed the black-and-white paintings of 1951, which many critics saw as both a retreat and a failure on the artist's part, it is worth noting that three individuals (the poet-critic Raphael Rubinstein, the art historian Hal Foster, and the museum curator Kirk Varnedoe) from very different quarters in the art world seem to agree on one thing: O'Hara's criticism does not warrant attention.

The primary, if largely unstated criticism of O'Hara's art writing is that it is too hyperbolic, too excited and uncritical. It is the opposite of serious and disciplined. Both a more judicious and a more careful reader, Berkson describes O'Hara's weaker pieces as being "self-consciously oracular," and states that under the pressure of deadlines his "prose stiffened" or became "constricted." The other problem is that O'Hara wore his heart on his sleeve when he wrote about art. In this puritan culture, readers (and other critics) are embarrassed by his excitement. How can you be an art critic if what you are looking at excites you? Being prone to excitement means that you lack restraint and are incapable of being scientific. The one writer who seems to have made the best use of this way of writing about art is Peter Schjeldahl, who is currently the art critic for the *New Yorker* (a job once held by the fustian Harold Rosenberg) and who has claimed that he no longer writes poetry. This is how Ashbery, who is not uncritical of O'Hara, saw his friend's relation to art:

> This art absorbed Frank to such a degree, both as critic for *ARTnews* and a curator at the Museum of Modern Art, and as a friend of the protagonists, that it could be said to have taken over his life.[20]

Here, Ashbery seems to be suggesting that O'Hara may have lost hold of the thread connecting him to his inner private life, that he became too externalized. While I won't dispute that O'Hara's writing was often excited and hyperbolic, I believe not only that he made many observations that are significant, but that he also took positions that continue to be instructive:

> Nevertheless, the viewer should make more distinctions than the artist, he has the time and room for it, he is merely looking and experiencing, where the artist is creating something, whether in his or another's image, no small feat in any case.[21]

O'Hara believes it is the viewer's responsibility to "make more distinctions," and to see each work for what it is, rather than how it might resemble someone else's work. And yet how many countless times, in reviews of both books and art, have critics either made a generalization ("painting is dead") or unfavorably compared one person's work to another's? Of course, the point behind such comparisons is to elevate one person's work at the expense of another's. O'Hara found this behavior unseemly. His nonhierarchical approach to art, to what he called "the living situation," is what distinguishes him from other critics. It is the opposite of what most people think a critic is supposed to do, which is to criticize and judge, make hierarchies. One may believe these hierarchies are based on something more "scientific," but they are hierarchies nevertheless. O'Hara takes a different tack and challenges the public to both look more closely and read more carefully. He wants viewers (and this includes art critics) to locate their understanding of art in their actual experience, rather than in a predigested idea about what they are looking at. He is challenging us to suspend judgment and start fresh with each work of art we encounter.[22]

As Ashbery pointed out in his introduction to the *Collected Poems,* O'Hara's poetry was "anti-literary and anti-artistic," which suggests why he liked the art that he did. Being anti-artistic means you are anti-formalist (unlike the art historians writing for *Artforum*), but it doesn't mean that you are against formal mastery. This is what O'Hara has to say about Pollock's *Blue Poles: Number II* (1952), a late painting which, because structural elements ("blue poles") are used to organize the unruly, clotted field, many art historians see as evidence of the artist's precipitous decline. For them, Pollock has introduced figural elements into his painting, and backed away from allover abstraction. In contrast to the formalists who believed abstraction was the highest development and representation of any sort was a step down, O'Hara offered this appraisal of Pollock's controversial painting:

> *Blue Poles* is our *Raft of Medusa* and our *Embarkation for Cythera* in one. I say *our,* because it is the drama of an American conscience, lavish, bountiful, and rigid. It contains everything within itself, begging no quarter; a world of sentiment implied, but denied; a map of sensual freedom, fenced; a careening licentiousness, guarded by eight totems native to its origins (*There Were Seven in Eight*). What is expressed here is not only basic to his work as a whole, but it is final.[23]

This is exactly the kind of writing that drives Foster and other art historians up the wall and over the other side. They see it as a prime example of fustian babble, whereas I see it as both metaphorical and analytical, poetic and precise, but I want to make clear that it is very different from poetic prose. I am not talking about the dreamy fictions of Anais Nin here, but about O'Hara's compressed summation of a painting by Pollock. If I have a problem with O'Hara's description, and I do, it is that it is too compressed. It requires the reader to unpack it, and recognize the connections that the writer is making. I think the reason O'Hara wrote this way is because he believed, either naively or willfully, that the reader knew as much, and felt as passionately about culture ("living situation") as he did. For O'Hara, art history was as much a part of the present as Chinese poetry was for Ezra Pound and the archaic was for Guy Davenport.

O'Hara connects *Blue Poles* to Theodore Gericault's *Raft of Medusa* and Antoine Watteau's *Embarkation for Cythera* because he recognizes the many affinities that these three artists and their cited works share. In terms of biography, Watteau (1684–1721), who was frequently ill, died of tuberculosis at the age of thirty-seven; Gericault (1791–1824), who was injured while riding a horse, died at thirty-two; and Pollock (1912–56), who was killed while driving a car, died at forty-four. They were young men in the prime of their artistic careers. In terms of the reception their art received, it should be remembered that Watteau's training was unconventional, and that his paintings did not fit into any of the established categories. In fact, in order to acknowledge Watteau's accomplishment, the French Academy invented a new term, *fetes galantes,* to describe his wistful, nonnarrative paintings. When Gericault's *Raft of Medusa* was first exhibited, it caused a controversy not only because it disregarded classical conventions, but also because it was considered too morbid in its subject matter. Like Watteau and Gericault, Pollock challenged the established conventions that society relied on to define a painting. Willem de Kooning described Pollock as the one who "broke the ice," which could also be said of Gericault and Watteau. All of them were groundbreakers whose work was not immediately accepted. Thus, the three paintings O'Hara connects together are thought of as flawed masterpieces. By not elaborating upon these connections, the poet hurts his own case. There is, however, a precision to his art writing. It isn't simply a matter of him free-associating, and writing down whatever pops into his head. O'Hara may not be the greatest prose stylist in his essays on Pollock, but we don't read Meyer Schapiro for style, do we?

By connecting *Blue Poles* to the American psyche ("a map of sensual freedom, fenced"), O'Hara takes the painting out of the museum and situates it in something as messy as culture. He looks at the painting as if he were Alexis de Tocqueville looking at America. Doesn't his "lavish, bountiful, and rigid" fit right in with de Tocqueville's understanding of democracy? Both men possess innocence and insight. They see what is right in front of everyone's eyes, but which others haven't noticed.

One reason William Carlos Williams hated T. S. Eliot was because he felt that he had returned poetry to the classroom. O'Hara believed that a painting's ultimate destination was the world, not the museum as a sarcophagus or pristine resting place. He didn't think of art as a precious object meant to be sequestered from everyday life. Strong art doesn't need the protection of a sterile environment; it can live in the world. That's what makes it crucial. O'Hara even wrote glowingly about the Guggenheim Museum, a museum whose interior design many dislike:

> Anyhow, I like the whole experience, the "bins" where you come around a semi-wall and find a masterpiece has had its back to you, the relation between seeing a painting or a sequence of them from across the ramp and then having a decent interval of time and distraction intervene before the close scrutiny: in general my idea is that this may not be (as what is) the ideal museum, but in this instance Frank Lloyd Wright was right in the lovable way that Sophie Tucker was to get her gold tea set, which she described as, "It's way out on the nut for service, but it was my dream."[24]

Who else but O'Hara could connect Wright and Tucker, the high and the low? He had a wonderful sense of humor about the situation in which he was active. As much of an aesthete as he was, and he was down to the soles of his feet, he was also a poet who chose to live in the world. He didn't want the security of academia because, I suspect, he knew it would stifle both him and his poetry. This is how he described the elevator at the Guggenheim:

> The elevator is a good idea, too; I wonder if anyone has ever taken it down? And apart from the one-way thing, it takes off the curse of most elevators, which is that when you go up in an elevator you are usually going to some unpleasant experience like work or a job interview, but here you are going up for pleasure.[25]

This is the challenge O'Hara presents to other poet critics: Can writing about art be both demanding work and real pleasure? And if it can be that, then doesn't the act of surviving in New York City become inextricable from the pleasure of what it offers in museums and galleries?

It is safe to say that John Ashbery has published more articles and reviews in self-supporting magazines and periodicals than any other poet of his or subsequent generations. In contrast to O'Hara, whose reviews appeared in *ARTnews* and in little magazines such as the *Evergreen Review, Horizon, It Is,* and *Kulchur,* Ashbery largely worked for publications that were read by a middlebrow public. Week after week, and over a period of many years, he produced highly informative articles and reviews for the *Herald Tribune, New York,* and *Newsweek.* Thus, in its heterogeneity, the readership for Ashbery's criticism is very different from those who would have read O'Hara's chronicles in little magazines. One might assume that the reason O'Hara's writing could be so hyperbolic was because he knew an informed, largely sympathetic audience was reading it, while Ashbery knew from the outset that he was writing for strangers. Despite this difference, what Ashbery and O'Hara share is a nonhierarchical approach to the art world, which, I want to emphasize, doesn't mean that they didn't repeatedly stand for and against something.

As a critic working within the art world, Ashbery had to become a commentator whose range of interests, enthusiasms, and preoccupations was recognized, in all senses of the word, by both the reader and those in positions to commission articles and reviews. The Scylla such a critic faces—and I suspect one must address this early on in one's career—is how to resist the temptation to become a social Darwinist who writes approvingly about those whose work has already achieved success in the marketplace. It is not about going against the tide so much as ignoring it, about not letting the outer reality become yours. In what ways can you contribute to and perhaps even inflect a world that is not necessarily open to being challenged or criticized? How do you proselytize without becoming proscriptive, dogmatic, or polemical? Certainly it is tempting to become publicly programmatic when you see few if any apparent results from your writing, to elect to become both a knight and a martyr. For if you have avoided Scylla (the role of social Darwinist,) you (who are always a proselytizer even when writing about successful artists) also have to bypass Charybdis, which is the exciting prospect of becoming judgmental, opinionated, argumentative, and self-righteous, particularly if you are championing those who are not at, or perhaps even near, the center of the art world's fickle attention.

The art world is full of curmudgeons, each more sanctimonious than the next. Curmudgeonliness is an efficient way of getting attention, and being remembered. For the rest of us, it is a guilty pleasure because we feel both sympathetic and superior to the bile-spewing critic, and get a vicarious thrill from all that chest-thumping self-righteousness. We secretly like watching people making fools out of themselves in public, all the more so when they can do it expressively. It is why clowns entertain some of us.

If these obstacles aren't enough, the successful poet-critic, which is to say one who regularly gets published, will most likely be dismissed or ignored by art historians, theorists, academics, and, in some cases, other poet-critics. In addition, being a successful art critic and published poet means that you have to accept that more people will read your criticism than your poetry. And if this isn't enough, it also means that you realize that the American literary establishment is apt to take your essays seriously only if you write about literature or culture or are from another country and write in English, but will regard your writing about art as akin to reviewing romance novels for a supermarket tabloid. It takes a certain kind of resiliency to be a poet critic who not only doesn't become a curmudgeon, become polemical, stop writing poetry, or start complaining about the inequality of it all, but also still manages to maintain a high level of sophistication, insight, and wit in your essays and reviews.

About the art criticism of Ashbery, the question boils down to this: what does he stand for and against in his essays and reviews? I would like to approach this question by beginning with a distinction he makes in an essay about Artaud:

> His famous pamphlet on Van Gogh (*Van Gogh or The Man Suicided by Society*) is great not because Artaud was a great critic (which he wasn't because fortunately he could only create, not criticize) but because of what it says about all artists.[26]

This is what Ashbery says about artists and the critic's relationship to them: "To create a work of art that the critic cannot even begin to talk about ought to be the artist's chief concern."[27] He is championing art that exists outside of language, particularly when it is academic discourse. It might make his job tougher, but he is against any kind of art that can be explained by a preexisting discourse. Thus, in this same review of Brice Marden's monochromatic paintings, he writes: "it is not an abstraction but an object made by and for the senses."[28] This observation is in line with his statements about art and poetry that are "life-like," and that move between the conscious and the unconscious.

Ashbery is an heir to Walter Pater, who proposed that all art "aspires to the condition of music." The difference is that Pater is seen as paving the way for abstraction, while Ashbery began publishing poetry and criticism after abstraction's triumph. Thus, he wants an abstract art that is an object made by and for the senses. In other words, he isn't interested in abstraction as an idealized state, but in something messier and closer to life. He believes in art and writing that are autonomous but not removed from reality. This is why many find it nearly impossible to write about his poetry; it keeps slipping through one's fingers and reconstituting itself just beyond one's grasp. It isn't constituted around themes, those little engines that poets often use to get them from line to line.

While Ashbery isn't particularly interested in criticizing an artist's work, one should not deduce that he wasn't critical of artists, because he was, but in a way that can only be described as creative:

> Leland Bell is a painter and a polemicist. Seeing him in his studio, vigorously at work on a number of canvases and meanwhile sounding off on his various pet peeves and enthusiasms, one has the feeling of coming upon an almost extinct variety of whooping crane, alive and well in its environment, happily honking around the pond and causing quite a commotion. For polemics, and by extension commitment—to art, that is—is all but extinct in the art world. Where polemics seems to flourish, it often turns out to be the wishful thinking of artists dedicated to the hopeless task of doing away with the art of the past, and must therefore be construed as a romantic metaphor rather than a practical exercise in persuasion.[29]

What is striking about Ashbery's irreducible view of Bell is that it is simultaneously comical, critical, cold, entertaining, and even sympathetic. After all, none of us wants to see any animal, particularly a whooping crane, become extinct. Clearly, the tonal shifts and multiple voices that are an integral part of Ashbery's poetry are also found in his essays. Even though many of his essays are assignments and commissions that appear in art magazines and weekly journals, he has an original prose voice. He isn't afraid of using a rich complex metaphor or citing a popular term. He isn't a miser who feels compelled to hoard his metaphors for his poems.

One wonders why, in his review of *Selected Prose,* Charles McGrath made this observation:

> On the evidence of "Selected Prose," in fact, it's tempting to conclude that prose is something Ashbery isn't especially good at, which makes him unusual among poets of his stature. Seamus Heaney and Derek Walcott, to take the two most obvious examples, are brilliant critics and essayists, with prose voices as original and as pleasing as their poetic ones. Ashbery's prose writing is clear and competent (he worked as a journalist and art critic for many years) but also dutiful and uninspired. Most of the pieces in this volume are the equivalent of literary chores—and from them you get no sense of how much fun Ashbery can be or what a master of tone and voices he is, able to shift gears in a single line. Most of "Selected Prose" is written in an all-purpose monotone.[30]

On the evidence of McGrath's review, one is tempted to conclude that he never read *Reported Sightings,* and that being, as his byline describes him, "the former editor of the Book Review and a writer at large for The Times" means you don't have to have know a whole lot more about your subject than the average reader of your publication. McGrath's observation, which I don't think is atypical, is just one more bit of evidence that, when it comes to a poet, particularly one who is considered avant-garde, the American literary establishment finds it difficult to honor its own.

Written more than decade before the emergence of appropriationists, a number of whom were championed by Hal Foster, Ashbery's observations regarding polemics have a particular relevance in both the art world and literary culture. One doesn't think of what appropriation artists such as Mike Bidlo and Sherrie Levine do as being a "romantic metaphor," and certainly that is not how their work has been framed and written about by art historians involved with postmodern pronouncements regarding the death of originality and the death of the author. And while it certainly wasn't on his mind when he wrote this in 1970, nearly a decade before the emergence of Language poets and others who (influenced by European theorists) proclaimed the death of the author, as well as mounted heated arguments against the use of the word "I," it should be noted that Ashbery's use of "I" is unlike that of any other poet. Ashbery's "I" is porous and changing, and the reader doesn't sense that it is connected to a fixed personality, as it is in the writing of James Tate, Charles Simic, or Jorie Graham, just to name three obvious examples. I would further suggest that something of the personality of such poets as Bruce Andrews, Charles Bernstein, and Leslie Scalapino comes through in their work. Thus, whether one uses or doesn't use the "I," or publicly believes in or doesn't comment on the death of the author, isn't really the point, is it? Making statements about these issues is really a way of announcing to others what club you belong to or are trying to be admitted to. In contrast to the poets I have just cited, Ashbery writes without an agenda.

Influenced by contemporary art—and here I am thinking of Jean Hélion and Jasper Johns (two artists he has written about)—Ashbery has submerged his personality in favor of something that is seemingly objective and distanced. His description of Johns's work seems particularly applicable to his own poetry:

> Johns is one of the few young painters of today whose work seems to defy critical analysis, and this is precisely a sign of its power—it can't be explained in any other terms than its own, and is therefore necessary.[31]

For more than four decades, Ashbery has defined, defended, and championed the difficult and unexplainable, not because he is "a harebrained, homegrown surrealist,"[32] but because he recognizes that the beginning of modernism, which is marked by the poetry of Baudelaire and the painting of Manet, is manifested by the collapse of a collective language. How can you be edifying when there is no collective language or set of symbols to rely on? Within this situation of absence, particularly of moral authority, the writer has two choices: write poems as if there still exists a collective language or try and write poems that achieve complete autonomy. Ashbery chooses the latter.

Both T. S. Eliot and Ezra Pound tried to construct a collective language, however gloomy or willed, but Ashbery never tried to achieve a didactic totality. Thus, in his poem "Into the Dusk-Charged Air," one named river replaces another, and there is no sense of landscape (context) or use of the word "I." Reality is indifferent to us, and its constant, relentless change carries us along, whether we like it or not. Each of us begins in the middle of it:

> Far from the Rappahannock, the silent
> Danube moves along toward the sea.

Without fanfare, Ashbery often challenges some of our most cherished views of art. In his essay on Edwin Dickinson, which appeared in *New York,* he makes the following observation:

> Coming on this show fresh from the Whitney's [Edward] Hopper retrospective made me wonder once again if we really know who our greatest artists are. I would be the last to deny Hopper's importance, but even in the smallest and most slapdash of these oil sketches, Dickinson seems to me a greater and more elevated painter, and all notions of "cerebralism" and "decadence"—two words critics throw around when they can't find anything bad to say about an artist—are swept away by the freshness of these pictures in which eeriness and vivacity seem to go hand in hand, as they do in our social life.[33]

Hopper, of course, is the artist everyone points to when they want to prove that a collective language of representation still exists. It is Hopper who, many fervently claim, most powerfully evokes our urban isolation and alienation, which is all well and good. At the same time, meaning has been detached from Hopper's paintings, making them into a background against which a very programmatic conversation can unfold. Hopper is easy to sum up, while it is impossible to do so with Dickinson.

However, without ever denying Hopper's importance, Ashbery brings up "eeriness and vivacity" as aspects of our "social life" we might want to pay more attention to. Hopper hints at his figures' inner life, but everything we see takes place on the painting's surface. This is why so many mainstream poets have used Hopper's paintings as a starting point. With Dickinson, however, it is all but moot to discuss what constitutes inner and outer reality.

One of the painters whom Ashbery became friends with while living in Paris was Jean Hélion, whom he championed many times. A provocative, commanding painter who challenges one's assumptions about art, Hélion worked both abstractly and figuratively, and did not "attach much importance to the two categories." He is impossible to categorize, and, in that way, is comparable to Philip Guston. The difference is that Hélion worked in four different modes of abstraction before shifting to figuration; he was both more stylistically restless and less seductive than Guston. Like Guston, Hélion tried to deal with dailiness after he moved away from abstraction.

A friend of Raymond Queneau and Francis Ponge, Hélion also published *They Shall Not Have Me* (1943), a memoir about his experiences as a POW in World War II. His letters to Queneau are full of bright gems about art. He wrote poetry before switching to painting. In the late 1920s, he became known for his abstact paintings that excluded "lyricism, drama, and symbolism."[34] In the early 1950s, Hélion, who, by the way, was a big influence on Leland Bell and his polemical stance, began working on "fanatically realistic still-lifes." Writing about these works and a portrait he was working on, Ashbery concludes his essay on Hélion with this note:

> As he once said: "I realize today that it is the abstract which is reasonable and possible. And that it is the pursuit of reality which is madness, the ideal, the impossible.[35]

It so happens that there is a retrospective of Jean Hélion currently on tour. It opened at the Centre George Pompidou, Paris, and will have stops at the Museu Picasso, Barcelona, and the National Academy Museum, New York. The accompanying catalog contains essays by French, English, and American art historians. However, Ashbery's early championing of Hélion—and he was pretty much one of the only American critics to do so—seems to have made no impression on any of the historians, and none of his writings is included in the English version of the catalog.[36] This is just another example of a lost opportunity.

Being a poet and art critic means that much of your writing will appear in fugitive publications, in small magazines, middlebrow magazines with a short shelf life, and catalogs that only a few people will ever see or read. Most of the people who read the poetry probably won't read the essays about art and vice versa. The mainstream literary establishment won't pay much attention and that part of the literary establishment that thinks it is avant-garde or radical also won't pay much attention because art, after all, makes money and therefore must be corrupt. The art world still largely ignores poet-critics. And yet, despite the absence of attention in this area, and even though nobody might have bothered to notice, it must be apparent by now that Ashbery does take positions in his art criticism and literary essays, and that throughout his publishing life he has articulated them with remarkable clarity and precision. It seems not to matter to Ashbery whether or not someone reads what he writes about art. He would take a stand even if no one were listening. That, I believe, is the definition of integrity.

NOTES

1. *John Ashbery in Conversation with Mark Ford* (London: Between the Lines, 2003), p. 43.

2. In contrast to many of the other Abstract Expressionists, Bradley Walker Tomlin (1899–1953) moved in both the commercial world and downtown bohemia. He was both a successful illustrator and a painter. He designed covers for *Vogue* and *House and Garden.* In the last five years of his life, Tomlin used a vocabulary of ribbon-like calligraphic strokes, which are the temperamental opposite of Franz Kline's crashing slathers of paint. Both Philip Guston and Robert Ryman have admired Tomlin's tonalities and delicate, matter-of-fact, structural brushstrokes.

3. John Ashbery, *Reported Sightings: Art Chronicles 1957–1987,* ed. David Bergman (New York: Knopf, 1989), p. 193; first published in *ARTnews* (Oct. 1957).

4. John Ashbery, *Selected Prose,* ed Eugene Ritchie (Ann Arbor: University of Michigan Press, 2004), p. 15; first published in *Poetry* 90, no. 4 (July 1957).

5. Ashbery, *Selected Prose,* p. 21; first published in *Evergreen Review* 4, no. 11 (Jan.–Feb. 1960).

6. Ashbery, *Selected Prose,* p. 22.

7. Ashbery, *Selected Prose,* p. 22.

8. Ashbery, *Selected Prose;* first published in *New York Times Book Review,* June 1, 1969. For those who are interested in the degree to which Ashbery has dissolved the distinction between inner and outer realities, I would recommend they compare the early poem "The Instruction Manual," which makes a clear distinction between these two realms, to his recent poem "Interesting People of New Foundland," where one is unable to apply such distinctions.

9. Helen Vendler, "Ashbery's Aesthetic: Reporting on Fairfield Porter and Saul Steinberg," *Harvard Review,* no. 22 (Spring 2002).

10. Marjorie Perloff, *Frank O'Hara: Poet among Painters* (New York: George Braziller, 1977).

11. In addition to being an art historian, Michael Fried is a poet whose books include *To The Center of the Earth.* His forthcoming book is *The Next Bend in the River.* For those who wish to know more about Fried as both poet and art historian, see the poet and critic Barry Schwabsky's astute review "Makeshiftedness," *London Review of Books,* Apr. 17, 2003.

12. Hal Foster, "Art Critics in Extremis," in *Design and Crime* (London: Verso, 2002), p. 108.

13. Foster, "Art Critics," p. 108.

14. Manny Farber's essay "White Elephant Art vs. Termite Art" (1962) is one of the best critiques of the art world's loyalty to the "gemlike inertia of an old, densely wrought European masterpiece." It also continues to be ignored by many art historians.

15. While I myself am not personally acquainted with such poets, I have been assured by many trustworthy individuals that there are numerous poets like this, and that many teach creative writing in prestigious universities all across America, and have received national recognition. I have also been told that these poets encourage their students to choose a similar path, and cultivate their sensitivities while sequestering themselves from the harsh vagaries of the world.

16. When I mentioned Foster's caveat about poet-critics lacking a paradigm, the poet Robert Kelly responded: "Oh I have a paradigm, I just can't fit it through the door."

17. Raphael Rubinstein, "Preface," in *Polychrome Profusion: Selected Art Criticism 1990–2002* (Lenox, MA: Hard Press Editions, 2003), p. 11.

18. Hilton Als, "Frank Appraisal," *Artforum* (Oct. 1999).

19. *Jackson Pollock,* exhibition catalog (New York: Museum of Modern Art, 1967). The show started in New York and traveled to Los An-

geles. In his afterword to *What's with Modern Art,* by Frank O'Hara, Bill Berkson's clear-eyed assessment of O'Hara's art criticism is at odds with Raphael Rubinstein's blanket judgment. Berkson's generosity, sympathy, criticality, and insightfulness, all of it articulated in beautiful prose, are also evident in his book *Sweet Singer of Modernism* (Providence: Qua Books, 2004), which collects a number of essays, including exemplary ones on Wayne Thiebaud, Alex Katz, and Piero della Francesca.

20. John Ashbery, "Introduction," in *The Collected Poems of Frank O'Hara,* ed. Donald Allen (New York: Knopf, 1971); reprinted in Ashbery, *Selected Prose.*

21. Frank O'Hara, "Art Chronicle," in *Art Chronicles 1954–1966* (New York: George Braziller, 1975), p. 5.

22. In this regard, O'Hara and Ashbery have aligned themselves with the positions taken by the art historians Meyer Schapiro and Leo Steinberg. They base their conclusions on looking, rather than theory.

23. O'Hara, "Art Chronicle," pp. 37–38.

24. O'Hara, "Art Chronicle," p. 2.

25. O'Hara, "Art Chronicle," p. 2.

26. Ashbery, *Selected Prose,* p. 32; first published in *Portfolio and ARTnews Annual 2* (1960).

27. Ashbery, *Reported Sightings,* p. 214; first published in *ARTnews* (Mar. 1972).

28. Ashbery, *Reported Sightings,* p. 213.

29. Ashbery, *Reported Sightings,* p. 195; first published in *ARTnews* (Feb. 1970).

30. Charles McGrath, "Mapping the Unconscious," *New York Times Book Review,* Mar. 6, 2005, p. 10. McGrath reviews both *Where Shall I Wander* (New York: Harper Collins, 2005) and *Selected Prose.*

31. Ashbery, *Selected Prose,* p. 69; first published in *ARTnews* (Mar. 1966).

32. Ashbery, *Selected Prose,* p. 164.

33. See Ashbery, *Reported Sightings.*

34. From the manifesto authored by Theo Van Doesburg that appeared in *Art Concret,* no. 1 (Apr. 1930) p. 1.

35. Ashbery, *Reported Sightings,* p. 65.

36. Although I haven't been able to verify this, I have been told that an essay by Ashbery is reprinted in the French and Catalan versions of the catalog.

"Feelings Are Not Quiet"

Life & Death, by Robert Creeley

Of all the outstanding poets belonging to the generation born around 1925—John Ashbery, Allen Ginsberg, Barbara Guest, Denise Levertov, and Frank O'Hara—Robert Creeley is the least poetic, the one who has most successfully resisted employing metaphors and similes to propel his poems. Not only are his poems unadorned, but much of the language he uses is neutral. And yet, despite the numerous arguments made to the contrary, Creeley is no more a minimalist than Jasper Johns is a Pop artist. Putting aside the obvious differences in their media, and given that Creeley's ostensible subject is love and domesticity, and that Johns's is the changing relationship between the individual's mind and body, both men have far more in common with each other than with their devotees. In addition to recognizing that our fundamental isolation from each other is inextricably linked to the changes caused by time's passing, both Creeley and Johns take great pains to make their work exist in the same world as that of the reader and viewer. How then to look at the impending chaos without blinking is what these two men have repeatedly asked themselves in their work of the past two decades. The results are bracing.

For all of Creeley's resistance to the poetic, he has never been programmatic in his approach to language. Rather, as one who is deeply sensitive to how much is presumed in the use of language, he is skeptical of the ability of words to ground him

Review of *Life & Death,* by Robert Creeley. From *Boston Book Review* (1998).

in the actual world, its unfolding here and now. Creeley's skepticism helps explain why Language poets hold him in such high regard. But many turned this skepticism into a platitude that enabled them to bypass any encounter with the so-called personal. And yet, I would argue that Creeley has accomplished something far more challenging and radical than exploring themes associated with the death of the self. In his renunciation of the poetic, he has not only exposed the presumption of the oracular, prophetic thrust of American poetry, but he has also rejected the romanticist notion that the poetic self is a more sensitive, more elevated state than that experienced by the ordinary individual. In this regard, poets of all stripes may have failed to grasp the essential current running through all of Creeley's work. He refuses to speak for us, refuses to believe he has something to teach us about life, society, or language; "I know I constitute only a meager voice and mind." This isn't modesty, it is wisdom.

Creeley never presumes to be in control of the poem, no more than he is in control of his thoughts, feelings, or the world. Since *Pieces* (1969) and *A Day Book* (1972), when he moved away from what Denise Levertov called the "ravishing perfection" of his earlier, tautly chiseled poems, Creeley has become increasingly open to various impulses, fluctuations of thoughts and feelings, in his attempt to register the daily passage of his life. *Life & Death* brings into succinct focus Creeley's recent concerns. Divided into three sections, the book's twenty-seven poems include "Histoire De Florida," a nearly twenty-page chronological sequence of journal-like observations and meditations, "Signs," a series of dense, echoing, punning prose poems, and "Inside My Head," a rhymed sequence of nine-line poems. If any of us had any doubts, such formal variations should make it clear that Creeley, who, in addition to his poetry, has written a novel, short stories, a radio play, criticism, and other less identifiable prose, is one of the most restless poets of his generation. He may be of "meager voice," but he is not of meager ambition.

"Histoire De Florida," the book's opening sequence, articulates Creeley's perceptual shift from perceiver to the perceived. The first section of this twenty-page poem reads:

You're there
still behind
the mirror
brother face.

Only yesterday
you were younger,
now you
look old.

Come out
while there's still time
left
to play.

It is difficult to imagine language plainer than this. And yet, Creeley isn't anti-poetic; it's that he so much wants the words he uses to locate him in, as well as bring him to, the changing present. From the surprise and wonderment in the first stanza, he moves to the second stanza, which pivots from a laconic moment of self-reflection ("Only yesterday / you were younger) to a terse, un-self-pitying observation ("now you / look old"), articulated in quick staccato. The shift in line length and music conveys a change in tone and feeling.

Common to Creeley's strongest poems is the way he synthesizes the musicality of the lines with the pauses and line breaks to register shifts in mood, perception, and focus. A range of complex emotions comes through; it literally surfaces if we read attentively enough, acknowledging the hesitations caused by the placement of caesurae, while being aware of the pauses and shifts caused by the line breaks. Reading becomes an enactment in which, through the sonorous medium of language, we move in tandem with the poet, and are carried along with him, even as the experience is often bleak and he offers no easy comfort, no way out. In one section, midway through "Histoire De Florida," he interrupts his memory of a well-known line from Wordsworth, "Emotions recollected in tranquillity . . . ," and asks, "which is what?" and then without hesitation goes on to list:

> Feelings are not quiet, daughter's threatened
> kidney's, sister's metal knee replacement, son's

vulnerable neighborhood friendship, Penelope's social
suitor's, whom I envy, envy,
Age. Age.

Wordsworth's "tranquillity" is at best an ideal, at worst a cliché. One cannot step away from one's life.

In "Signs," a sequence of interconnected prose poems, Creeley explores the widening gap between the aging body and sexual desire, imagination, and memories. If what we do in our heads isn't something we can necessarily do with our bodies, where do we live? What are the thoughts that suddenly flood the mind? What do they tell us? Where do they lead? Where does the "I" live? What or who constitutes this "I?" These are the questions Creeley repeatedly confronts in his work. Thus, the second prose poem transforms, inverts, and echoes the first prose poem ("The old ones say, 'The peach keeps its fuzz until it dies'"):

> It begins with I stand there. The old ones say, "The speech keeps its fizz until it dries." For years and years one never grew up, never first or last. But was like a river rather, a dark whoosh, and there was at last one old anticipated on the dark bank, *I* stands there in my pajamas. Shouts, *apple, stone hard's got! Hands wrought, God's bought-bodies!* The sky is ground at bottom.

Growing older, the world is literally and figuratively being turned upside down; and there is nothing Creeley can do about it.

In "Mitch," Creeley, remembering a close friend and his feelings of helplessness, regret, and anger in the face of that friend's death, narrows his focus, as if the light itself is leaving the room:

I should have hugged him,
taken him up, held him,
in my arms, I should
have let him know I was here.
Is it my turn now,
who's to say or wants to.
You are not sick, there are
certainly those older.
Your time will come.

In God's hand it's cold.
In the universe it's an empty, echoing silence.
Only us to make sounds,
but I made none.
I sat there like a stone.

Not only do all those soft and hard *o* sounds in the last stanza evoke a sigh, a release of one's breath, but the last line ("I sat there like a stone") anticipates Creeley's own future, even as it registers a moment of extreme isolation and paralysis. But at no point does Creeley make claims on the reader's sympathy. Rather, he knows his grief cannot be shared or dissipated, that it is his and his alone. This is why I think his work is so central, why it's a touchstone for those who are struggling with what it means to be both human and a member of a community. Creeley doesn't present his experience as either representative or special. He is never didactic, never acts superior, and never shows off. I can't think of many poets who have such implicit faith in both the reader and language's materiality, its substance. Knowing that language offers no refuge from time, that it does not enable one to transcend one's circumstances, Robert Creeley deserves our praise and heartfelt thanks for being so much in the world we inhabit, but hardly share. Few of us have the courage to do so.

Robert Creeley and Georg Baselitz's *Signs*

In its marriage of language and image, *Signs,* a collaborative book project between the American poet Robert Creeley and the German artist Georg Baselitz, feels both inspired and right. Living in Europe in the early 1950s, initially in France and then in Majorca, Creeley first saw the work of Jackson Pollock in Paris. In Pollock's work and that of other Abstract Expressionists, Creeley recognized that a number of painters had made "a shift" he himself "was anxious to make," which was to move from the pictorial or imagistic to a process rooted in the materials themselves. As Creeley understood it, Pollock had established a direct, unbroken connection between the means (content) and the end (form).

In 1961, while Baselitz was living in West Berlin, where he had arrived four years earlier from East Germany, he coauthored the *Pandemonic Manifesto 1, 2nd Version* (1961). Full of visceral imagery and harsh, staccato rhythms, the *Pandemonic Manifesto* was influenced by the writings of Antonin Artaud. By choosing Artaud as an influence, Baselitz openly identified himself with poets for whom blasphemy was a necessary aspect of their writing. Thus, for both Creeley and Baselitz, it was work in another medium that proved crucial to their development.

As made amply evident by the exhibition "In Company: Robert Creeley's Collaborations," Creeley's projects with visual artists challenge any assumptions we might have about both the *livre d'artiste* and the nature of collaborative endeavors involving

---

Review of *Signs,* by Georg Baselitz and Robert Creeley. From *Art on Paper,* vol. 4, no. 6 (July–Aug. 2000).

a poet and an artist. A prominent member of a brilliant generation, Creeley is certainly the only poet of a groundbreaking group, which includes John Ashbery and Frank O'Hara (1926–66), to have made collaborative projects a central aspect of his writing process.

The project was initiated by printer, poet, and master printer Hank Hine, the director of Graphicstudio, a collaborative workshop at the University of South Florida. As the publisher of the San Francisco–based Limestone Press/Hine Editions, Hine had also devoted considerable attention to the *livre d'artiste.* Among the sixteen books he had published under his imprimatur, Hine had initiated, overseen, and published *Winter* (1992), a book of fourteen etchings by Baselitz accompanying a fourteen-stanza poem by the Nobel poet Joseph Brodsky, and *Parts* (1994), a book of nine mezzotints by Susan Rothenberg for which Creeley wrote nine poems.

In writing nine poems for Rothenberg, each directed toward a specific print, Creeley reveals his commitment to working within the parameters established by the artist. Creeley's method is significantly different from what Frank O'Hara, collaborating with Larry Rivers, did in *Stones* (1957–60), where, in a playful dialogue, both poet and artist worked directly on the lithographic stones. In *Stones,* words and images are inseparable, as they merge with as well as interrupt each other. By contrast, in *Parts,* as in other collaborations in which Creeley has participated, the poet's writing stands on its own, even as it is intimately connected to the artist's work. It is Creeley's determination to establish a relationship, which is simultaneously attentive and self-sufficient, that distinguishes his collaborations from those of O'Hara and other poets.

In *Parts,* Creeley wrote a poem for each of Rothenberg's mezzotints, with the imagery of the poems echoing the artist's austere, ghostly images of human and animal body parts. Baselitz's work, his inverted world, provoked a very different response from the poet. After seeing Baselitz's work, and visiting and spending time with him in his studio in Germany, Creeley wrote "Signs," a prose poem consisting of a numbered sequence of sections. In its use of puns, echoes, and shifting scenes, "Signs" is formally analogous to the artist's upside-down, collapsing world.

In both the subject matter and formal construction of "Signs," Creeley makes poignant parallels to Baselitz's upside-down world. He recognizes Baselitz's characteristic inversions as analogous to his old age, thus connecting the artist's formal device to his own deepening awareness of mortality. Echoing in language Baselitz's visual reversals, Creeley uses echoes, rhymes, puns, and repetitions to convey the instability of language. In doing so, language, which forms the very ground of our thinking and communicating, becomes shaky, almost groundless.

The first section reads in its entirety:

> The old ones say "the peach keeps its fuzz
> until it dies." It seemed for years as if one
> would never grow up, never be the first
> or last to say anything. But time is like a
> river, rather, a dank, sluggish rush, and here
> one is at last as anticipated old on its nether
> bank. I stand there bewildered, in my pajamas,
> shouting, "The stone is an apple before its
> got hard. *The ground is the bottom of the sky.*"

Seeing his inverted reflection in time's unstoppable river, its "dank, sluggish rush," the poet is "bewildered," disoriented. His world has been turned upside down: "*The ground is the bottom of the sky.*"

One of the tensions running throughout the sequence is the poet's intense awareness that, while his body keeps getting older, he remains subject to memories (the past) and recognitions (the present) that make him all the more conscious that time's passing (the future) means his inevitable absence. In the fifth section, he writes: "I lied when I told you I was lying. Clean sheets for dirty bodies, God's dotties, odd's potties." In following a linguistic paradox with insistent, nonsense-like repetitions, Creeley masterfully evokes the alpha and omega of our contact with language, childhood nursery rhymes and senility, a coming into language as well as a losing of one's grip on it and how it is used. Rather than writing about old age as if he is observing it from some safe vantage point, Creeley connects language's materiality, and the continually shifting relationship between sound and meaning, to his own awareness of the body's materiality and decay. "Signs" reveals how we live inside language and are unable to either escape or transcend it.

After reading what Creeley sent him, Baselitz was finally able to make etchings to accompany each of the numbered prose sections in the sequence. For although he first read Creeley's poems in translation in the early 1960s, "Signs," with its puns, inversions, and lack of overt narrative, proved understandably difficult for him to understand. Rosmarie Waldrop, a highly regarded poet and translator from German and French, as well as a former teacher of Hine and friend of Creeley, graciously provided Baselitz with explanatory notes.

In the etchings, Baselitz sets one kind of mark-making against another, hard ground and soft ground, by repeatedly juxtaposing a deep black, linear element (hard ground), usually a cropped image of a naked, falling figure or body part (feet, hands, head), with a red and green image of a fruit or flower (soft ground). By combining a harsh, black, linear element with one that is porous and in color, Baselitz conveys a primal world at irresolvable odds with itself. Marrying a specific technique to a particular image reminds us that while there is one world, human beings and fruits and flowers exist in it differently. Most notably, fruits and flowers exist in cyclical time, while humans are caught in linear time. Finally, however representational the drawing, Baselitz never tries to disguise the essentially abstract nature of his marks. Everything is clearly either a deeply cut, linear mark or a softer area of color.

In his choice of technique and imagery, Baselitz is extremely attentive to Creeley's poems. One senses that he chose to work the way he did because he wanted the etching, both formally and imagistically, to mirror Creeley's attentiveness to language's materiality, the way it sounds as well as means. Acknowledging the remarkably astute, formal equivalents that Creeley and Baselitz made in response to each other's work, Hine used equally sized copper plates to print both the prose poem and the etchings. Paired on facing pages, the etched poem and the etched image mirror each other in myriad ways.

Creeley's involvement in *Signs* did not stop with his writing of dense blocks of prose. He worked with Hine on both the size and the kind of type he wanted. For him, the clarity of the typography, as well as the readability of the text, were of utmost importance. He wanted something that was both direct and bold, but which worked in seamless harmony with Baselitz's images. In his caring about the way the physical book actually looks and feels, one senses that the thing itself is of major concern to the poet. The book must function as a book, as something that can be read and looked at. As Creeley understands it, if a collaboration is to be at all successful, it must be the result of different individuals, in this case a poet, artist-printmaker, and publisher-designer working together to make something that is larger than any one sensibility. It is a communal project, as well as evidence of a community's existence. *Signs* is such a book.

Philip Lamantia

In 1944, the teenage Philip Lamantia (b. 1927) was invited by Andre Breton to join the Surrealists. The only American poet ever to be welcomed into the Surrealist movement, Lamantia single-handedly transformed its language of incommensurability into a far wilder and far more disruptive American possibility. Lamantia was an isolated figure in American letters, and his poetry has quietly influenced poets for more than four decades, most recently Will Alexander, Garrett Caples, Jeff Clark, Andrew Joron, and John Olsen.

Although Lamantia's youthful poems were influenced by Surrealism's reconciliation of opposites ("The mermaids have come to the desert"), they are unlike anything else that was being written in America during the 1940s. They owed nothing to Ezra Pound and William Carlos Williams or to the strain of English poetry that includes Gerald Manley Hopkins and Thomas Hardy among its predecessors. One can't imagine W. H. Auden, Marianne Moore, or Robert Lowell writing, "As the women who live within each other's bodies / descend from their polar regions / to the circle of demons. . . ." Not even poets such as Robert Bly, Charles Simic, and James Wright are capable of such oracular utterance.

Lamantia's association with the Beats marks the second phase of his career. And while they received far more attention than he did, Lamantia's independence was unrivaled. He didn't need public adulation and didn't know how to make small talk. While others made pronouncements, he "read the spells of Egyptian patiently." In the early 1950s, in San Francisco, he met Lawrence Ferlinghetti, who would later start City Lights Books

---

From *Boston Review* (Oct.–Nov.1997).

and bookstore, and, starting with *Selected Poems,* published four of Philip's books between 1967 and 1997. According to Ferlinghetti, Philip was "writing stream of consciousness Surrealist poetry, and he had a huge influence on Allen Ginsberg. Before that Ginsberg was writing rather conventional poetry. It was Philip who turned him on to Surrealist writing. Then Ginsberg wrote 'Howl.'"

By the late 1950s, Lamantia had synthesized Surrealism's oppositions and demotic American speech: "No one completes a sentence I am in hell to complete it." Full of out-of-print work, *Bed of Sphinxes: New and Selected Poems 1943–1993* (1994) reminds us that there has always been an alternative to Language poetry's emphasis on the materiality of words, as well as to mainstream poetry's belief in the objective poem that possesses an authorial "I" at its center. (The poetry of Jack Spicer and John Ashbery are two other, very different alternatives.)

Lamantia's domain is the heightened and even ecstatic state of consciousness. His poems are hallucinatory and disembodied; they connect the visible to the invisible, the occult to the everyday, the cacophonous present to the dark mythic past: "Gemmed, caught up in the old ways, silver flesh / gleams between mandibles of the African Kingfisher / These moving realities appear on the Nile / as if a postcard view of it held up a hieratic bird." Even now, more than fifty years after he first began publishing his poetry, Lamantia's flights of language are unlike anyone else's. For what this poet does in his synthesis of language and the body is achieve a heightened, ecstatic state in which the disembodied self is undergoing a miraculous metamorphosis.

Archie Rand's *The Letter Paintings*

I.

Between 1967 and '71—starting when he was seventeen years old—Archie Rand (b. 1949) worked on *The Letter Paintings,* a thematically related series consisting of more than one hundred paintings, some of which are more than fifty feet in length. Both in their scale and in their incorporation of a constantly changing, cursive linearity, the paintings are a clear indication that the youthful artist was more preoccupied with Jackson Pollock's legacy than with securing an exhibition. What dealer, much less one in his or her right mind, would exhibit paintings by a teenager that are fifty feet in width? Even now, more than thirty years after he completed the series, Rand's project conveys a monumental ambition, which makes the subject of these works all that more poignant.

The recurring focus of *The Letter Paintings* is the names of black musicians, singers, and composers, most of whom were (and still are) unknown, as well as song titles ranging from doo-wop tunes to bebop improvisations. Mixed in with these names are the names of baseball players, minor and neglected artists, and young poets and writers whom Rand knew and was hanging around with at the time. While Rand was in some sense documenting a particular milieu, which consisted of writers and artists and their passion for music and baseball, this certainly was not all that was on his mind. We no more look at Rand's *The Letter Paintings* for their names than we read Frank O'Hara's

---

Exhibition brochure, Allen Priebe Gallery, University of Wisconsin-Oshkosh (1997).

poems for theirs. Both men created works that, for all the names they mention, go far beyond that.

Rand worked on unstretched bolts of unprimed canvas, which enabled him to make the paintings as wide as he wanted. Depending on what he was doing—developing a ground or drawing the letters—he would place the canvas on the floor or affix it to the studio wall. He used acrylic, sometimes mixing it with a homemade gel, which resulted in different consistencies, ranging from a liquid line to a thick, frosting-like surface. Often, the frosting-like surface appears petrified, as if the cake has been kept in the freezer a little too long. He used traditional and nontraditional tools, such as brushes, cake combs, rollers, squeegees, pastry tubes, magic markers, ballpoint pens, and mops. He used spray cans to paint names with enamel. At times, he drew with his fingers. The hothouse palette adds another emotional layer to the frosting-like surface.

II.

In their subject matter and palette, *The Letter Paintings* are decidedly urban and share something with what seems their opposite, the black-and-white paintings of Franz Kline. Kline's milieu is Manhattan in the 1950s, while Rand's is New York (all the boroughs) in the late 1960s and early '70s. Kline's paintings are contiguous with the rise of documentary photographs, while Rand's paintings are made in a world becoming immersed in television, Technicolor, and Cinemascope, and their weird, not quite right color. The paintings' expansive scale evokes both the panoramic landscape of the Hudson River painters and the movies, particularly westerns. The grand embrace of space one associates with these two mythologizing views of America is double-edged.

For one thing, Rand has written the names of people hardly embraced by America then or now: the writer Gilbert Sorrentino; the German painter August Macke, who was a battlefield casualty in World War I; avant-garde jazz musicians Cecil Taylor and Eric Dolphy; and doo-wop groups long since forgotten, Pookie Hudson and the Spaniels, The Marvelettes, The Cadillacs, and The

Orioles. Many of these figures have achieved a cult status but not what Warhol would call their fifteen minutes of fame.

Seen (and now remembered) against the nightly news postings of those who died in the Vietnam War, not to mention those dying in urban riots or being assassinated, Rand's lists evoke, among many other things, the gap between anonymity (death) and recognition (fame). Rand was seventeen and almost draft age when he started *The Letter Paintings,* and in that sense they are autobiographical. If his name was to be on a list, he might have thought to himself on more than one occasion, perhaps the list could be made of paint rather than newsprint. If his life were brief, maybe a stranger would remember him. What would August Macke have done had he lived longer? he might have asked himself.

Each of Rand's lists of names constitutes a self-sufficient system of information or what we now call data. His juxtaposition of the names "Jules Olitski" and "Fantin Latour" in a single painting, all of it done in florid colors, can be understood on a number of levels. By placing in close proximity a contemporary painter whose work was being promoted as radical and avant-garde and a painter noted for his depictions of flowers, Rand initially seems to be both paying homage and being critical, and even ironic. However, I think the painting offers a deeper reading than the surface one of irony.

For while the juxtaposition suggests that Olitski and Latour are interchangeable, and the tropical colors imply that both are makers of decorative paintings for a self-satisfied household, I would also propose that Rand doesn't feel inherently superior to either artist. There is nothing quick or smug in the way he has painted their names, which are about the same height. Both names have been lovingly drawn out. It is equally obvious that the artist has affection for the florid palette.

Rand started his project during a period when many observers had declared that painting was dead, and aligned himself to some degree with the color field painters and formalism (he was the studio assistant of Larry Poons during this time). In *The Letter Paintings,* Rand asked himself what it meant to believe in painting and painters. For if you do believe in them, and you have invested your faith in the culture of art, on what grounds would you establish a hierarchy that separated one artist or kind of painting from another? Isn't hierarchy about an external set of values? In *The Letter Paintings,* Rand is working out his argument with both color field artists and the formalist critics who were their advocates. At the same time, through *The Letter Paintings,* Rand begins separating himself from, as well as challenging, the milieu which had first welcomed him. He is using the paintings to make a space for himself, a task all young artists and writers must take up.

One of the underlying reasons for Rand's separation is, I would suggest, the formalist reading of Pollock that still had cachet in the art world. In 1965, in an influential exhibition catalog, Michael Fried proposed that Pollock's work signaled a historical progression toward dematerialization and "opticality."[1] A bookish man who is deeply and widely read, Rand would have known Fried's essay, and been familiar with his and other formalist arguments. In *The Letter Paintings,* he takes on both Pollock and the formalist reading of his work directly. His response to Pollock is to extend his abstract, cursive linearity into writing, as well as to use an acrylic medium that runs from looping visceral lines to thinly applied script. While Cy Twombly "desiccated what had been fluid in Pollock's manner," Rand slowed the fluidity down, made it possess a very different consistency.[2] He didn't pour or dribble the paint, he squeezed it from a pastry gun or tube.

The writing, particularly who and what it references, makes explicit the urban feel of Pollock's paintings. At the same time, Rand transforms the expansiveness and evocation of infinite spaces of Pollock's poured paintings into an obsession with naming, which is implicitly exponential and boundless, while shifting the aerated surfaces into a field that is simultaneously visceral and optical.

III.

The logic of Rand's choices is particular to each painting, which makes the paintings quite distinct from each other. He isn't interested in seriality or variations on a theme. Rather, he is rooted in the specific to such a degree that he wrote the names of all the sidemen who played in Count Basie's and Duke Ellington's orchestras of the '30s and '40s. He made silly rhymes and associations, such as pairing Wyndham Lewis and Jerry Lee Lewis, Duke Snider and the Duke of Earl. He placed the names of Fats Waller, Wilbur Ware, Thurston Harris, Lavern Baker, and Fontella Bass in his paintings at a time when the Rolling Stones, who had learned a lot from black music, particularly the blues and R&B, had gained an immense amount of attention in all the media, and their every move was reported in the news. While the Stones and other groups contributed to both the revival and the long overdue recognition of many black musicians and songwriters, the original figures remained marginalized for the most part. They were the opening acts rather than the headliners.

Rand's one guiding rule was that he refused to write out the names of superstars such as Elvis Presley and The Beatles; they were already famous and needed no more attention. In this, Rand's paintings share something with the paintings of Ed Paschke from the 1960s and '70s. Both artists focused their attention on outsiders and marginalized figures, individuals who for one reason or another would never be assimilated into or by mainstream culture. In this sense, the paintings of Rand and Paschke are implicit critiques of Andy Warhol's silkscreen paintings of Presley, Marlon Brando, Jackie Kennedy, Marilyn Monroe, and Elizabeth Taylor.

That Warhol's silkscreened celebrities are celebrated as quintessential American paintings, while Rand's lists in gaudy colors and Paschke's jarring portraits of losers and outsiders have achieved a cult status, says a lot about the art world's need to replicate mainstream culture's determined blindness. It seems to me that if we really want to understand something about America and American painting of the 1960s and '70s, as well as gain insight into our present situation, a room in which one could see the paintings of Warhol, Rand, and Paschke together would be helpful. Certainly, it might cause us to think differently about the work of all three artists, and I think that can only be useful. The compartmentalization of art according to style enables us to be satisfied with identifying, rather than looking. It helps preserve the status quo.

IV.

In retrospect, what *The Letter Paintings* make abundantly apparent is that Rand established his working method while he was still a teenager, and that he merged his flexible, open-ended method with a wide range of interests, which he has continued to engage on a deep level. Throughout his career he has remained a devoted student, which is to say he is obsessively thorough, deeply inquisitive, extremely patient, and precise. In this regard, he shares something with Jasper Johns, Robert Ryman, and Charles Seliger, three classic autodidacts. Given Rand's sense of being Jewish, it can be said that he is talmudic in his approach to painting, in terms of both materials and subject matter.

It is also evident that Rand has resisted confining his ambition to that of a gallery space. Three years after he finished *The Letter Paintings,* Rand painted the cinder-block interior of Congregation B'nai Yosef, located on Ocean Parkway and Avenue P, Brooklyn. In order for it to cover over thirteen thousand square feet of space, this project, which preoccupied the artist from 1974 until '77, required an immense amount of research, as well as the artist's working with various people to develop a synthetic polymer that wouldn't fade or distress over time. In 1984, Rand painted over three thousand square feet of exterior murals on the walls of Jerusalem Teacher's College.

Along with these and other large mural projects, all of which required long hours of research, planning, and negotiation, Rand worked on a number of series in which he responded to specific literary texts. In 1987, he completed *The Sonnets to Orpheus (Part II),* based on Rilke's sequence. In each of the twenty-nine paintings, one for each sonnet, Rand did a self-portrait, which interacted in unpredictable ways with images inspired by a specific poem in the sequence. On the back of each painting, he wrote out the sonnet that he had used as inspiration. *The Sonnets to Orpheus (Part II)* is predicated on Rand's belief that he could become the Orphic figure, the receiver, through which Rilke spoke in images, in paint.

In 1991, Rand did fourteen paintings based on the sequence of poems Jack Spicer published in *The Book of Music.* Spicer believed that poets took "dictation," and early in his career wrote a sequence of poems, "After Lorca," in which the "ghost" of Lorca tells him what to write. While this way of working can be connected to Rand's love of musicians such as Charlie Parker, who did improvisations on well-known tunes, it also defines a widening of the sense of authorship and originality. In 1995, he did a series of twenty-four paintings, *Men Who Turn Back,* based on a sequence Eugenio Montale wrote after his wife, Mosca, died. Montale, it should be noted, based his series on a series of poems Thomas Hardy wrote in 1912, shortly after his wife died. Lineage, as Rand's various bodies of work imply, is something you create, it is a web of associations.

In 2001, Rand completed a collaboration with John Ashbery. *Heavenly Days* consists of forty-seven paintings largely done in Payne's gray and unbleached titanium white, which the artist has said is the same color as "parchment." Occasionally, Rand mixed in a different black. All of the views in the series are of the interior of the poet's house in Hudson, New York. The title comes from a long poem by Ashbery. In each painting, the poet has written lines from the poem, which makes *Heavenly Days* his only active collaboration with a visual artist.

The trajectory of Rand's career resembles no one else's, and it can only be described as idiosyncratic. I don't mean stylistically weird, because he is not being willfully eccentric. Rather, Rand works on projects that stand at a great distance from each other. I can think of no other artist who works quite in this manner. At the same time, beneath the very real and immediately apparent distances separating one project from another, one senses that Rand is preoccupied with the relationship between word and image, and that his preoccupation may have its origins in the Bible, particularly Genesis. I suspect that what unites Rand's seemingly very disparate bodies of work is his ongoing interrogation of faith, what it means to believe, which was very much on his mind when he started *The Letter Paintings.*

From another perspective, one senses that Rand understood Pollock's abstractions differently than his contemporaries. As a teenager, he worked on paintings whose scale dwarfed Pollock's largest paintings. In his mid-twenties, and after he finished *The Letter Paintings,* he took on the project of painting the cinder-block walls of Temple B'nai Yosef. In doing so, he extended the implication of Pollock's mural-sized paintings, as well as returned murals to their original function as public art.

At the time of *The Letter Paintings,* Rand was a student at Pratt, studying, among other things, cartoons. What I have not mentioned is that along with the projects I have touched upon, he has done many paintings and series of paintings in which the format is based on the panels one associates with cartoons. Rand's interest in cartoons is one proof that he is not working out of a collage aesthetic, which is how I would characterize the work of David Salle (b. 1951), for example. Rather, Rand's aesthetic is one in which image and language dance around each other. It is an aesthetic that explores the slippery disjuncture between image and language, between what is said and what is seen.

V.

Despite the claims of critics and theoreticians that the seductive power of the mass media pulls us into an immense, inescapable empty space, a numbing simulacrum, *The Letter Paintings* challenge that paradigm of postmodern culture. Assimilation (and thus exchange) is not possible for everyone, and the parodies, subversions, and alternatives that both individuals and marginalized groups make manifest are not finally acceptable to mainstream society. In both recovering and exposing a part of American cultural history that has been covered over, as well as in transforming the disembodiments we associate with color field painting into a visceral opticality, Rand has created a significant and engaging body of work. It is time to recognize these paintings for what they are: a challenging, exuberant, celebratory, and elegiac body of work. *The Letter Paintings* praise cultural workers of all kinds, even as they mourn their passing into death or obscurity. Starting in 1967, a young artist transformed his love for both music and Pollock's lyric chaos into an obsession with naming, witnessing, and remembering, and asked for acceptance and respect for the many people whose names he had written. The result is a large body of original paintings.

It is a very human thing that Rand has done. Isn't it time that our response be human rather than ideological, expansive as the works themselves, rather than compartmental?

NOTES

1. Michael Fried, *Three American Painters: Kenneth Noland, Jules Olitski, Frank Stella* (Cambridge: Harvard University Press, 1965).

2. Kirk Varnedoe with Pepe Karmel, *Jackson Pollock,* exhibition catalog (New York: Museum of Modern Art, 1998), p. 68

Street Song

The Art of Jean-Michel Basquiat and the Poetry of Kevin Young

I wanted to be a star, not a gallery mascot.
—Jean-Michel Basquiat (1960–88)

Grace to be born and live as variously as possible.
—Frank O'Hara (1926–66)

I.

The birth of modern Paris, its broad boulevards and glassed-in arcades, penetrated the work of the artists and poets who witnessed the changes. Amidst this shift in consciousness, the birth of modern art and poetry took place. Paris permeates the poems of Baudelaire, the paintings of Gustave Caillebotte and Edouard Manet. Writing of Baudelaire, Walter Benjamin points out that "the Chthonic elements of the city—its topographical formation, the old deserted bed of the Seine—doubtless left their impression on his work."[1] In more ways than one, Baudelaire absorbed aspects of both the new and the old worlds into his work.

A hundred years later, the center of the art world shifted from the rushing crowds and glassed-in arcades of Paris to the maelstrom of sights, sounds, and cultures colliding on New York's streets. Its topography of steel bridges, elevated subways, and gritty, graffiti-covered walls is echoed in the charred blacks and sooty off-whites of Franz Kline and Willem de Kooning. In New York, particularly during the 1950s and '60s, artists and poets

---

Two Cents, exhibition catalog (Miami: The Centre Gallery, 1996).

hung out together, drank, talked, and argued at the Cedar Bar and other downtown watering holes, as well as collaborated on various projects.

Frank O'Hara collaborated with Larry Rivers on a set of lithographs, *Stones,* and with Norman Bluhm on *Poem-Paintings.* On the weekends, O'Hara, Rivers, Bluhm, and other artists and poets would go to the Five Spot and listen to Thelonious Monk, Charlie Mingus, or whoever was playing or singing that night. In his poem "The Day Lady Died," written just three years after the Supreme Court ruled that "separate but equal is not equal," O'Hara memorializes Billie Holiday. In a country where segregation was still the law, a white man wrote eloquently about his admiration for a black woman. One was a poet, the other a singer.

In some places in this world, there are people willing to cross the lines maintained by society, knowing that there is a price to pay. And in those places—both the art world and the literary world are similar in this respect—to cross the line often means to demand respect and acceptance. Jean-Michel Basquiat crossed many lines, but, despite all the attention he received in his short life, respect and acceptance didn't come to him until after he died.

Notoriety isn't all that it's cracked up to be. Jean-Michel Basquiat was always more notorious than he was famous, which is to say he got a lot of attention for the wrong reasons. Many critics were unable to forget that Basquiat didn't attend art school—something he, Joseph Cornell, Jasper Johns, and Robert Ryman have in common—and that he first gained attention for his graffiti tag, SAMO(c).[2] These critics fail to address the fact that in his paintings Basquiat worked as an autodidact, someone who studied his subject, which was black history, both attentively and thoroughly. That he was black was another reason for his notoriety, the other being that he was photogenic, two facts also common to the poet and editor Kevin Young. But, as both of them knew early on in their lives, surface is death and, to live with any measure of dignity, one must get beyond the surface, and not be trapped in the mirror society uses to hold you in.

Jean-Michel Basquiat was born in 1960, the year Kennedy was

elected president, and died of a heroin overdose in 1988, the year Reagan left the White House. Kevin Young was born a decade later, in 1970, at the height of both the Vietnam War and race riots, and published his first book of poems, the prize-winning *Most Way Home,* in 1995, the year America normalized relations with Vietnam. The book's dedication reads, "For my family–blood, adopted, imagined."

Although Young graduated from Harvard and Basquiat dropped out of high school, they could have, and most likely would have, met, given the overlap in their mutual affections. Although separated in age by a decade, they share many common interests: music, particularly bebop and blues; Hollywood movies and the history of race they embody; both the public and the elusive underground history of art; the largely untold history of black America; and the daunting gamut language runs, from the ivory tower to the mean streets, and from feel-good clichés to comic book expletives.

Beyond their affections, what Basquiat and Young share is an understanding of language's continuum. They are streetwise polyglots, keepers of both the demotic and the highfalutin. They are conversant in the slippery terms and tongues that dwellers in the chaos of America's urban sprawl use to communicate among themselves and, when need be, with others from a different street or neighborhood.

Young's dedication suggests one reason why he began writing about Basquiat at some point after *Most Way Home* was accepted for publication but before it was published.[3] He recognizes that Basquiat is a member of his family. While his poems about Basquiat can be said to extend out of his earlier concerns, they are also both a disruption and an eruption, a significant development in this young poet's work. In them, Young has stood narrative on its head and shaken it hard. Moving away from both story and linearity, which are characteristics of the poems in *Most Way Home,* he started cobbling together puns, explored shifts of meaning, and used comic book speech, repetition, and multiple voices.

The slippery, destabilized nature of language, as it is embodied in the urban sprawl, becomes the ground out of which Young's poems emerge. Instead of the smooth transitions and single "I" one finds in the poems in *Most Way Home,* Young's recent poems are full of rapid juxtapositions, typographical shifts, imaginative equivalents of urban slang, and graffiti-like shorthand. The poems mix together eulogy, celebration, fable, history, and biography in an attempt to set the record straight. Young wants to recuperate Basquiat, make him come back to life.

Writing about the young dead John Keats in his elegy "Adonais," Shelley admonishes the reader, "Peace, peace! he is not dead, he doth not sleep— / He hath awakened from the dream of life. . . ." When someone's life is cut short, it isn't only a time for grief and tears; it is also a time for anger, a time for closely examining both the self and society. And, as Shelley made apparent, it is a time for unleashing the power of incantation. Shelley believed that magic and the incantatory power embedded in words could bring Keats back to life. In his poems for, and about, Basquiat, Young concurs.

Henry Geldzahler once asked Basquiat, artist and heir to Surrealism, Art Brut, and the influence of the Spanish poet Federico Garcia Lorca, "What is your subject matter?" Basquiat answered: "Royalty, heroism, and the streets."[4] On the surface Basquiat's answer is that he is going to bear witness to the noble lineage of his family tree ("blood, adopted, imagined"), to acts of extraordinary human dimension, and to the chaos of urban life where tall stories, piecemeal tales, sightings, lamentations, raps, odes, and songs are constantly bubbling up.

For Basquiat, survival, self-destruction, and art go hand in hand. In his work he lists those who survived (Miles Davis, Dizzy Gillespie) and those who didn't (Charlie Parker, Jack Johnson). Are the ones who survived heroes? If so, are the ones who died young, or were denied their day in the sun, victims? Or are these questions at best moot? Can there be a clear division between right and wrong, and between yes and no, when one's perspective is shaped by a society that dumps people on the streets, like extra baggage? Is anything about our life simple?

As Basquiat sees it, royalty and heroism are possible only when an individual gives something back to the streets. His first gifts were as a graffiti artist intent on disrupting our lives with messages that we didn't immediately understand. As Basquiat knows but doesn't say to Geldzahler, his being a witness is tempered by his understanding of the history of the black male body and the passage from Africa to America, from warrior-kings to slavery, and from rulers to servants. Basquiat wants to make that unspoken, effaced history visible. He wants to confront the viewer with his art as he once confronted the pedestrian with his graffiti. He wants to both disturb and affirm.

In *Untitled (Crown)* (1983), Basquiat depicts a black three-pointed crown superimposed atop notepapers full of sketchy images and ramblings. In *Untitled (Notary Public)* (1981), he has written the words "Notary Public." The word "notary," as well as the crown icon, shows up a lot in Basquiat's work, sometimes followed by a copyright sign. A notary is someone empowered to acknowledge the signing of documents, a legalized witness.

Basquiat has empowered himself to be a witness to his own crowning. Knowing it is difficult enough for someone who is white and famous to be in control of his or her public image, and nearly impossible for someone who is black and famous to do so, he predicates his art on wanting to own both himself and the images of himself that he releases into the world. It is likely that he felt doomed from the start.

Occasionally, Basquiat copyrights "notary," as if he invented both the position and the word. Part logo and part memory of childhood, the crown is depicted with a generic, childlike simplicity. It's an ironic act, as well as an absurd gesture. Inhabiting Basquiat's knowing gesture is an air of calm desperation, street-wise reticence, and wise humor. For in a society where there is little place for you, except in certain designated areas, the logic of declaring yourself a legal witness to your own coronation makes sense in ways both ludicrous and ghastly.

No matter how much the art world honored him, Basquiat knew he would always be an outsider, would always be, in the eyes of many, "a gallery mascot." For the black male artist, dehumanization is all too often an inextricable part of the rise to fame, which suggests that the road from authenticity to commodity is measured in columns of media play. Whether black male artists (or poets, singers, athletes) want the responsibility or not, they know that the moment they step into the limelight cast by mainstream society, they will be intensely scrutinized because each will be burdened by the weight of being regarded as a representative of an entire culture.

It is within this milieu that Basquiat had to function as well as negotiate. His vision both challenges the status quo and presents an alternative. Neither cynical nor nihilistic, he genuinely believes that, at least within the realm of painting, he can crown himself, and determine how he is seen.

II.

Veering between fragmentation and discontinuity, Young's poems are propelled more by sound (puns, homophonic links) than by either narrative or the transparency of agreed-upon meaning. Words are both opened up and compressed to the point where a single word is doing the work of two or more. His poem "Hollywood Africans" begins: "Basquiat paints / the town." The separation between art (the act of painting) and life (celebrating and being celebrated by the media and the collectors who buy his work) is collapsed into a single terse declaration. The line is ironic. Young knows that Basquiat's life is shadowed by self-destruction, deep misunderstanding, distrust, and repeated folly.

Like many of the bebop musicians and Beat writers he so admired, Basquiat lived out beyond the reach of any safety net that might have saved him. For him, art and life were exactly as Young underscores: inseparable. This tragic fact gains in resonance when the reader/viewer recognizes that Young's title "Hollywood Africans" is from a Basquiat painting. Both poet and artist want to direct our attention to Hollywood, where supposedly art and life are separate realms. But the Hollywood of the 1930s and '40s (the subject of Basquiat's painting) was overtly racist both in and out of its films. And for the painter, the decision to separate art from life was not, as Young's poem makes clear, a simple option.

At the end of "Hollywood Africans," Young writes:

> SELF-PORTRAIT
> AS A HEEL #3. Hail,

hail, the gang's all
heels—no winners
or winters, just

wanderlust
among OSCARS (R)
& MOVIE STAR

FOOTPRINTS
like an astronaut's.
Rock planet rock

don't stop—POP
CORN—SUGAR
CANE. Academy

Mammy Award
& another for Butler,
Rhett—To the moon

Jemima—PAW—
Basquiat rockets
NEW!—hands pressed

fresh into pavement,
permanent as a rap
sheet, booked.

Using Basquiat's painting *Hollywood Africans* (1983) as a starting point, Young runs his own words together with words and phrases from the artist's paintings, the result being his take on both Basquiat's life and on Hollywood's treatment of black film stars. Beginning with a line in the painting (SELF-PORTRAIT / AS A HEEL #3), Young slides into a familiar song of camaraderie ("Hail // hail, the gang's all"), and then slides abruptly back to "heel," the originating word.

They may be in Los Angeles celebrating the opening of an exhibition, but Basquiat and his friends, the graffiti artists Toxic and Rammellzee, are still a gang to be exploited by others. For the collectors, some of whom work in the movie industry, these tough young artists (heels or bad guys) are both their latest prey (something they have stepped on) and most recent acquisition (pets who "heel").

Attentive to demotic speech, Young's sinuous twists and turns of language underscore how perilous it is to be a successful outsider in America. In Basquiat's case, the art world decreed that he was both a bad guy and something to step on, "a gallery mascot" or, as one reviewer stated, quoting a previous characterization, "a wild child raised by wolves."[5] This statement typifies society's self-protective need to infantilize the artist, to make him or her dependent on its largesse. Artists can be gifted, but they can't be adults. They are children in need of adult supervision (collectors, curators, and critics), which is one way society takes its revenge on artists. Whereas Basquiat wanted to give a gift back to the denizens of the street, the other outsiders, society wants the artist to understand that the only desirable gift, the only thing an artist should crave, is recognition by those perched in their moneyed nests high above the streets.

Young evokes Hollywood—the side that goes unseen and unmentioned—as a place where, if you're a black actor or actress from "the nineteen forties" (Basquiat's words), there are "no winners / or winters." For a white actor or actress, only the latter part of Young's statement (no winters) would be true. Young follows this observation with a brutally direct rhyme—"Academy // Mammy Award"—to bring the reader back to the time of *Gone with the Wind* (1939), the biggest box office hit in MGM's history, and the reception of Oscars by two of its stars, the white star Clark Gable and the black actress and singer Hattie McDaniel.

During the awards ceremony, McDaniel was segregated and sat alone at her table. Clark Gable might have played "Butler, / Rhett" but he wasn't treated like one, whereas McDaniel played a maid and was treated like one. She was the prototype for Aunt Jemima ("Jemima—PAW—"), the perfect black maid. McDaniel's award had a dual edge because her public life (her film roles as a maid and Academy Award) and her private one (her segregation and secondary or maid status) were inseparable. She couldn't be a hero in the movies because Hollywood would not have allowed it, nor would white America have accepted it.

By linking McDaniel with Basquiat, Young suggests that the actress's marginalized status echoes the artist's. Society would never allow either the maid and pet ("Jemima—PAW—") or the "heel" and ex–graffiti artist to put their handprints in the sidewalk outside Grauman's Chinese Theater. This honor is reserved for insiders rather than outsiders. Had Basquiat done so, he would have been "booked" for defacing public property, for returning to his roots as a graffiti tagger. The poem ends with Young again linking Basquiat and McDaniel, because "booked" means both to be charged as a criminal and to be hired as an entertainer.

In his use of "booked," Young is suggesting that for Basquiat and McDaniel, the option was to be either an entertainer or a criminal. Despite these obstacles, each has crossed a line and demanded but not necessarily gotten respect. McDaniel became an actress, but neither Hollywood nor America ever allowed her to transcend her roles as a maid. Thus, if McDaniel had tried to cross the color line and left her handprints in front of Grauman's Chinese Theater, she would have been "booked" as a criminal, rather than as an entertainer. By equating artists and entertainers with criminals and maids, Young comments on the roles society assigns to blacks. As Jasper Johns has so tellingly pointed out, "Artists are the elite of the servant class."

Young sees Basquiat's declaration—"SELF-PORTRAIT / AS A HEEL #3"—as proof that the artist is deliberately thumbing his nose at the collector and viewer, as well as flaunting his outsider status. Through his fracturing of language and thus surface sense, Young actively supports Basquiat's belief that the only meaningful gestures a black artist can make toward society must be both transgressive and subversive. Rather than allowing society to dictate both his behavior and options, something McDaniel, who belonged to an earlier generation, had to do, Basquiat wanted society to accept him on his own terms. He was transgressive out of necessity, rather than because it was a fashionable avant-garde option.

Both Basquiat's and Young's discontinuities (staccato rhythms, inversions of meaning, parodies of familiar phrases and tunes, harsh puns, shorthand, slang, obsessive lists of words, and quotes) parallel the improvisational music of Charlie Parker and Miles Davis. As in their solos, there is a subversive, shattering force driving Young's twisting narrative forward. By making words lose their securing ground, Young is able to gain a more compact and provocative cluster of meanings.

Young's poem doesn't describe Basquiat's painting in verbal

terms; the language isn't picturesque. At the same time, the myriad details and associations he has brought to bear are far too specific for the poem to be a variation on an abstract theme. Using polyglot bricolage and history, both poet and artist piece together fragments that have been suppressed, marginalized, or ignored.

III.

Not all the poems Young has written for Basquiat take as their starting point one of the artist's works. In "Charlie Chan on Horn," Young retells the story of Charlie Parker recording "a few sides" under the name "Mr Charlie Chan." The poem immediately begins with a disquieting double edge:

> For Prestige
>
> Bird records
> a few sides
> (for contract
>
> reasons) as Mr Charlie
> Chan—no matter
> the name his blues
>
> sound the same,
> same alto blaring
> ALCHEMY

Aside from being the name of a record company, "Prestige" means "authority of importance based on past achievements or reputation." It comes from the Latin *praestigia,* which means "deception." By both being true to the facts and ironizing the record company's brand name, Young brings a number of questions into stark relief. Does Parker gain his authority by deceiving us? And if so, what exactly is the nature of his deception? Or does he gain authority by recording under the name of Charlie Chan, a literary invention whose role in the movies is always played by white actors (Warner Oland, Sidney Toler, and J. Carroll Naish)?

What does it mean when Parker adopts the name Charlie Chan, who in reality is a white actor in yellow face? What does he imply when he steps into the role of a fictitious Hollywood character? Does he gain in stature by "passing" as Chinese? Is Parker suggesting that in America it's better to pass as Chinese than to be African American, to be yellow (or light brown) in color rather than black? To what degree are we aware of gradations of color, and how do we use them to distinguish one group or individual from another?

Without ever directly saying so, Young's poem reminds us that one of the manifestations of racism is the small distinctions that are used to isolate one individual or group from another. Part Haitian and part Puerto Rican, and growing up in a household where three languages (English, French, and Spanish) were spoken, Basquiat was always conscious of how he was read racially by others.

IV.

In "Vocabulario" Young accumulates a list of words beginning with the letter *c* in French, Spanish, and English, languages that Basquiat grew up with. By dividing the words up into three-line stanzas or clusters, the poet makes vivid Basquiat's relationship to language, as well as compels the reader to engage with the narratives they suggest:

cabal
caballero
cacao

cadaver
cafe
cambio

caramba!
carbon
caribe

Carmen
carnaval
carnivoro

catecismo
celebre
celibato

censor
centrifugo
cerveza

Cesar
cicatriz
ciudad

civilizacion
combustible
complexion

complice
conductibilidad
corazon

corroviso
cube
chimpance

chocolateria

The first stanza ("cabal / caballero / cacao") evokes a narrative consisting of "a small group of people organized to carry out a secret plot"; "a cowboy"; and the "tree from which chocolate, cocoa, and cocoa butter are derived." Thus, Young's three words should be considered in terms of both their etymology and the narrative their juxtapositions suggest. The reader doesn't read a story, but becomes conscious of the influence that history, one's time, and one's imagination have on language.

Are we to hear "cocaine" in "cacao"? Or are just we remembering the headlines about Colombia and its cabal of drug lords? Are we meant to recognize the collision of two different modes of production, cattle ranching and farming, in "caballero" and "cacao"? Or are we to consider how ranchers and farmers want certain advantages regarding the use of public lands? Instead of giving us a narrative we can easily consume, the poet reminds us that words, a "vocabulario," are defined by use, that they come with a history of uses and contexts, and that these uses and contexts have different meanings for different cultural and racial groups within America.

The fourth cluster of the poem—"Carmen / carnaval / carnivoro"—evokes the Brazilian Bombshell, the singer and dancer Carmen Miranda; the holiday marked by festivities, street revelry, masks, and pageantry, just before the start of Lent; and a meat eater. Also, "carnaval" literally means bidding farewell to flesh, to meat.

Like Hattie McDaniel and Anna May Wong, Carmen Miranda was a talented singer and actress whom Hollywood typecast. Usually filmed in extravagant costumes and campy headgear adorned with tropical fruit, Miranda became both a parody and a stereotype. Her official uniform was as much a part of her persona as McDaniel's maid's uniform and Wong's skimpy oriental dresses and strange, sculptural headgear were to theirs. Do we remember the religious significance of "carnaval," or do we think of it as a gathering of people in outrageous costumes? Is the surface what consumes our attention? Or do we want to see what lies beneath the glitter?

Throughout the poem, and with incredible economy, Young underscores the relationship between surface and depth, between the word and its etymological history. Each stanza embodies a slice of history; and each word reminds us that all words originate within a complex, cultural matrix. "Cacao," we might trouble ourselves to remember, comes from the Spanish via the Nahuatl. "Cabal" comes from the French via medieval Latin. Language, Young's poem makes clear, is not singular; it is multiple, and embedded within that multiplicity is a history of secret societies, conquests, trade, slavery, and betrayal.

On another level, "Carmen / carnaval / carnivoro" suggests a costumed performer, masks and celebrations, bidding farewell to the flesh, and the eating of meat. The history of food includes Christopher Columbus's search for a shorter passage to China and the spices and other food preservatives associated with the Far East. At the same time, "cacao" is the last word in the first stanza, and "chocolateria" is the last word in the poem. The poem begins with "cacao" (the source) and ends with "chocolateria" (the place where products derived from that source are sold). Civilization is predicated on transforming one material into another more valuable material. It is a process the artist reenacts when he or she turns paint and other materials into art. However, if we see that process as the only commodification (ironic or otherwise) of materials possible, the reader/viewer of Young's poems and Basquiat's art misses the point.

V.

Although Basquiat and Young never met, in the poet the artist has his most eloquent spokesperson. Young doesn't try to make the mess of Basquiat's life cohere into a single, overarching allegory. He doesn't settle for an easy and predictable music because, among other things, it would have been a betrayal of Basquiat, another exploitation.

William Carlos Williams said, "A new world is only a new mind." In "The Journey," the last poem in *Les fleurs du mal,* Baudelaire wrote, "Oh death, old captain, it is time, let us weigh anchor." The tragedy of Basquiat is that he confused Williams's "new mind" with Baudelaire's "depths of the unknown," living with dying, discovery with self-destruction. Given this society, and its emphasis on surface and the illusion of openness and upward mobility it works hard to maintain, it is understandable that Basquiat was drawn to the "depths of the unknown." Despite his short life, the triumph of Basquiat is that he articulated a history of the streets, its royal lineages and heroes, as well as documented a history that goes well beyond the personal. For any of us who have tried, we know that there is no sure path to the new world, no easy road that guarantees our arrival.

Basquiat's paintings and Young's poems are America's world, its tales of passage and of living in the diaspora. We are fortunate to have had one and now the other among us, showing us precisely the things we should hear and see—ourselves, and what we are making of this world.

NOTES

1. Walter Benjamin, "Paris, Capital of the Nineteenth Century," in *Reflections: Essays, Aphorisms, Autobiographical Writings,* ed. Peter De-

ment, trans. Edmund Jephcott (New York: Schocken Books, 1986), p. 157.

2. SAMO (short for "same old shit") was the graffiti tag used by Basquiat and his partner Al Diaz. It was often used to both start and give an added subversive dimension to a seemingly straightforward slogan: "SAMO; IF THEY SMITE YOU, TURN THE OTHER FACE."

3. Kevin Young, *Most Way Home,* National Poetry Series, chosen by Lucille Clifton (New York: William Morrow, 1995; rpt., Cambridge, MA: Zoland Books, 1999).

4. Henry Geldzahler, "Art: From Subways to Soho, Jean-Michel Basquiat," *Interview* 13 (Jan. 1983): p. 46.

5. Jeffrey Deitch, "Jean-Michel Basquiat: Anina Nosei," *Flash Art* 16 (May 1982): p. 49.

The Poetry of Jessica Stockholder's Titles

leaf autumn sky
flea umantu kys[1]

When Jessica Stockholder was ten, and growing up in western Canada, she went to her first poetry reading. The poet was bpNichol (1944–88). Known as "Captain Poetry," the legendary Canadian writer Nichol was a polymath. He wrote poetry, sound poems and concrete poems, songs and books for children. He taught, edited, and published *grOnk* (a visual-poetry newsletter). Committed to both the experimental and multiplicity, Nichol also designed new alphabets and wrote "novels" the length of a short story, operas, essays, and manifestos in different experimental forms. It would be easy to regard this childhood experience as an anomaly in Stockholder's life if she neither mentioned it[2] nor showed any understanding of both poetry and concrete poetry. Thus, it is useful to consider the following statement by Stockholder:

> The paint denies the thing that supports it and becomes an object of its own. But since paint doesn't exist physically as an object, it has to be attached to something; perceiving it as an object is an illusion, a kind of fiction. I like to create something emerging from what is concrete and known, from what we think of as real; to create a possibility for something kind of fantastic to emerge.[3]

Jessica Stockholder, exhibition catalog (Kunstsammlung Nordrhein-Westfalen, Dusseldorf and Stiftung: Wilhelm Lehmbruck Museum, Duisburg, 2002).

As Stockholder understands it, paint (like language) is contingent; and its existence is dependent on a support or context. Contingency is something she continually recognizes in her work. For nothing in either her installations or her small works is autonomous. Rather, they acknowledge their dependency. The small works, for example, are always connected to the wall by an electrical cord or a cord of some other kind.

Given that reality is made up of changing and shifting contingencies, Stockholder seeks to establish and explore a field of changing relationships in her work. For example, in her most recent installation, *On the Spending Money Tenderly* (2002), there are couches, places where one can see and be seen. Later in the same interview, Stockholder said:

> So I present fiction on an equal footing with material reality. I like that physical objects and events can seem continuous with the subjectivity of inner life. . . . Within this fiction, together with information and ideas carried by materials and with ideas expressed through the process of building, there is sometimes a kind of open narrative. This narrative can be understood as similar to the narrative in dreams viewed from a psychoanalytic perspective, where the meaning of any single element is in flux throughout the whole. I am also thinking of concrete poetry where the words on the page have both linguistic and visual meaning, and the power of the work comes from the two systems overlapping.[4]

One of the underlying tensions running through Stockholder's work arises from two conflicting recognitions, her desire to be true to reality, which is in a constant state of change, and her desire to be true to her materials, which, for the most part, are relatively stable. How does one reconcile instability and stability, the changing and the seemingly fixed? And, to return to her definition of concrete poetry, how does one make it evident in a nondidactic way that two systems are overlapping, in her case, sculpture and painting?

Instead of seeking reconciliation, Stockholder often includes organic matter (fruit and vegetables) in her installations. This is not just a comment on the tradition of still-life painting; it is also a reminder that time is passing and that one of the fictions surrounding art's status is that it achieves a permanent existence. Stockholder's installations are always temporary, and where they are situated plays an integral role in their construction. In *On the Spending Money Tenderly,* she makes conscious allusions to the open-air market near the museum. The museum after all is also involved in commerce and in helping to establish a value system; it is a kind of market where things are put on display, and in that sense verified and thus sold.

One reason Stockholder is committed to art that is temporary is because she recognizes that time pulls us all toward chaos and dissolution. In this regard, she shares something with Robert Smithson, who understood that entropy is inherent to time passing. Smithson placed *Spiral Jetty* in a lake, where it could be reclaimed by nature. In *First Cousin Once Removed or Cinema of Brushing Skin* (1999), Stockholder placed a truck trailer outside the museum, visible through the window and clearly part of the installation. The trailer underscored the installation's temporary nature, as well as reminded the viewer that a museum is not a final destination. In order to counter the museum's status as a mausoleum, a place where art is embalmed for all eternity, both Stockholder and Smithson incorporate fragility and entropy into their work without privileging or fetishizing them.

Given Stockholder's acute awareness of flux, and the fact that this awareness plays a central role in her installations, it is useful to consider how language functions in her titles, as well as the relationship between her titles and her work. Until the mid–nineteenth century, and the rise of Impressionism, titles largely functioned as a kind of frame or window. They named the subject one was looking at. James McNeill Whistler helped change this relationship between title and subject matter when he named a painting *Nocturne in Black and Gold—Falling Rocket* (1874), and called attention to the abstract qualities of the work. During the early part of the twentieth century, Kandinsky, Kupka, Malevich, and Mondrian all concluded that form and color were independent of subject matter. This resulted in their using titles in a very different way than their more representationally inclined predecessors. Kandinsky was the first to formulate the separation of form and color from subject matter; his titles include *Painting with White Border* (1913), *Several Circles*

(1926), and *Accompanied Contrast* (1935). Continuing this modernist tradition, Jackson Pollock began numbering his paintings in the late 1940s.

In a talk about Pollock that Stockholder gave at the Museum of Modern Art (December 1, 1998), during his retrospective there, she stated that she saw her first Pollock painting at MOMA while she was a teenager, and that it was probably *One: number 31, 1950:*

> Wondering now why that painting mattered to me I think about the huge thick volume that hovered out in front of the picture plane instead of inside it. The volume spoke to my body and to the painter's body. He used the picture plane as *a stage rather than as a window.* Everything pushed out into space. His process like mine was reactive. He moved through splotches of paint, bits of paper, sand. His action making the painting dragged through the material world and became material. And even so, I looking at the painting, was left with the feeling that something more than the sum of its parts was hovering between me and it. *That clashing of material with the ephemeral* is something I too am in love with. (Italics mine)

A number of writers have described Stockholder's installations as a stage on which the viewer becomes both an actor and a member of the audience. In such a situation the narratives one arrives at are open-ended. After all, there are no stage directions, no lines to recite, no story to memorize, and no preconceived plan as to how one should interact with the installation.

Stockholder's titles are equally open-ended. A number of them begin with a participle, an action in which the subject is not disclosed: *Making a Clean Edge* (1989), *Mixing Food with Bed* (1989), *Recording Forever Pickled* (1990), *Growing Candy Rock Mountain-Grasses in Canned Sand* (1992). By choosing to not designate the subject, the artist constructs a phrase that is synonymous with a continuous present. At the same time, the viewer becomes the subject of the phrase, becomes the one "making a clean edge."

Even among this handful of titles, one notices the artist's predilection for using both puns and aggregations of words whose sounds suggest other words. In "canned sand," for example, one hears "canned sound" (prerecorded music or

Muzak), while "mixing food with bed" perfectly echoes the cliché "mixing the good with the bad." At the same time, "grasses in canned sand" suggests a collision between nature and culture. Her titles suggest multiple, often incongruous readings, none of which is definitive. The inconsistencies of Stockholder's language clue the viewer to the likelihood that her titles mirror the flux at the heart of her art.

Stockholder destabilizes language, as well as subverts its accepted function as a window. In *Landscape Linoleum* (1998), which is a pairing of two words, one realizes that Stockholder endows each with equal value; they both affect how the other is read. There is the equation of exterior (landscape) and interior (linoleum), the possibility that landscape has become a kind of linoleum (something mass-produced), and the possibility that linoleum is for young children a landscape, and thus a far larger world than adults might presume. Echoing the viewer's role in her installations, the reader becomes the writer.

Stockholder's breakdown of the hierarchical aspects of language usage is comparable to a poet subverting both the habits of reading and the presumptions of meaning connected to that act. In *First Cousin Once Removed or Cinema of Brushing Skin* (1999), she makes an incompatible pairing that becomes even more so after a close reading. The "or" implies a choice, but what is it that we are choosing between? What does it mean to choose between a distant relative (a first cousin once removed) and an experience (cinema)? "Cinema of brushing skin" collapses a visual experience (cinema) with a physical intimacy (brushing skin). Is one the receiver or originator of the brushing? At the same time, the phrase "brushing skin" evokes both paint, where paint is a "skin" which the artist brushes onto a surface, and blushing or embarrassment.

Stockholder's titles are linguistic paradoxes; they convey unstable, open-ended situations that can be understood in different ways. One deduces from this imaginative use of language that she wants her titles to obliquely parallel one's experience of her installations. Thus, in both her titles and her installations, Stockholder wants the meaning to be unmoored, and to have no beginning, middle, or end. In talking about concrete poetry, Stockholder pointed out that the power of the work came from "two systems overlapping." This describes perfectly how her titles can be read. There is always at least a double reading.

The incompleteness of the title *On the Spending Money Tenderly* provokes the viewer into completing it in one of two ways: as "On the Subject of Spending Money Tenderly" or "On the Spending of Money Tenderly." Introducing the phrase "subject of" into the title makes the viewer the author of a treatise, the one who ponders what it means to spend money tenderly. And introducing "of" between "spending" and "money" makes one hyperconscious of the cliché "spending money," which suggests a limit to how much one can actually spend. Through both her title and her installation, Stockholder causes the viewer to focus on the relationship between money and tenderness. "Tender," we might remember, is another word for money. For Stockholder, one of the questions she wants us to consider is this: does a limited amount of money result in a limited amount of tenderness? And beyond this question comes another: in a society based on exchange and profit, how does tenderness get measured?

Stockholder's intent is neither to achieve a state of meaninglessness nor to purge meaning from her work. If anything, something close to the opposite is true. She wants meanings to accrue without privileging any one of them. In effect, she wants the meanings to be as open-ended and multiple as the work itself. And, in terms of the work, she wants the open-ended possibilities of meaning to be consistent with an individual's experience of the work, of walking through the installation, standing and looking at a situation that changes with each move one makes, and each direction one looks at. In constructing her titles and her installations, Stockholder mixes together words and things, which are unmixable. She compels us to question the way we read ourselves into the world.

NOTES

1. The pairing of "leaf" and "flea" should clue the reader that the rest of the pairings are also anagrams. "Umantu" is a Bantu word meaning "man," and "kys" is a homophone for"kiss"

2. In conversation with the author, New Haven, Sept. 18, 2002.

3. "Interview with Jessica Stockholder," by Eva Schmidt, *Jessica Stockholder* (Westfälischen Kunstverein Münster and Kunsthalle Zürich, 1992), p. 41.

4. "Interview with Jessica Stockholder," p. 42.

The Poet-Painters

Francesco Clemente and Nicola De Maria

I.

The term "Transvanguardia" was first used by Achille Bonito Oliva in the October 1979 issue of *Flash Art* to call attention to five young Italian artists: Sandro Chia, Francesco Clemente, Enzo Cucchi, Nicola De Maria, and Mimmo Paladino. Beyond their commitment to paint and to images, which distinguished them from the previous generation of more conceptually minded Italian artists, these artists had initiated a distinct and far-ranging dialogue with the history of art; and, in the case of Clemente and De Maria, this included Indian and classical Chinese art. Thus, the artists of the Transvanguardia had embraced aspects of art history which had been rejected or ignored by many older Italian artists.

Another contrast would be the younger artists' high regard for the Metaphysical artists and other early Italian modernists, a source of inspiration that many artists of the older generation had more or less rejected. By the end of the 1980s, they had superseded the term "Transvanguardia," which is as it should be; and each had become a highly regarded artist in his own right. At the same time, from the historical perspective afforded us by the passing of more than two decades since Oliva first used the term, one can revisit the original group and discern other, smaller constellations within it. For in revealing unforeseen connections as well as strong differences among them, time has

---

Transvanguardia, exhibition catalog (Castello di Rivoli Museo d'Arte and Skira, 2002).

exposed a very dense, rich network of affinities, connections, differences, and parallels to be explored.

The focus of my inquiry is Francesco Clemente (b. 1952) and Nicola De Maria (b. 1954). For while it is immediately evident that they are very different in both the intention and execution of their work, a longer, more engaged look at their respective endeavors discloses numerous affinities and parallels binding them together. The deepest affinity they share—and it is the one from which many others spring—is their connection to poetry. For them, poetry and language are essential elements of their work. In fact, I would argue that both Clemente and De Maria are poet-painters working within, as well as redefining and transforming, a dynamic tradition.

The tradition of the poet-artist—one could call it the "other tradition" in art—extends at least as far back as Chinese classical art and Wang Wei, of whose visual art nothing survives.[1] The eighteenth- and nineteenth-century visionaries William Blake and Odilon Redon belong to this tradition, as do seminal twentieth-century artists such as Paul Klee, Joan Miro, Henri Michaux, Francis Picabia, and Kurt Schwitters. Here it should be pointed out that along with Blake, Michaux, Picabia, and Schwitters wrote challenging, innovative poetry. Jean-Michel Basquiat (1960–1988) is another poet-painter. Finally, there are four older postwar artists more closely tied to Italy who have, in different ways and to different degrees, inspired Clemente and De Maria: Alighiero Boetti,[2] Mario Merz, Luigi Ontani, and Cy Twombly.[3] For all of these artists poetry is an important component of their work.

The two artists that have had an impact on both Clemente and De Maria are Ontani and Twombly. In 1957, Cy Twombly left America for Italy. In 1958, he had a show of paintings he had done in Italy at Galleria La Tartaruga, in Rome. In the brochure accompanying the exhibition, Palma Bucarelli suggested that the meandering pencil and crayon inscriptions in Twombly's paintings were the direct result of the artist opening himself up to the layers of graffiti found on Roman walls and monuments.

While Bucarelli's view is too simplistic and reductive, it does propose a direct link between Twombly's work and his circumstances. And while the link might now be regarded as tenuous and abraded, like the artist's lines, the connection Bucarelli made between Twombly's art and a world that is both ancient and daily was important for the permissions it would give a younger generation of artists. For in Twombly's work, Clemente and De Maria would see a world drawn over, erased, added to, and changed, a world of unmoored names and ceaseless naming, a world of sexual thoughts and fantasies, a world in constant flux.

What can be said about Twombly's paintings from the late 1950s onward is that formally they are both a continuation and a subversion of the gestural current found in Abstract Expressionism, particularly as it coalesced in Pollock's poured paintings. In Twombly's hands, Pollock's explosive, energetic line has become laconic, discontinuous, and desultory. A private diaristic sensibility is introduced into the field of painting. Doubt and fantasy replace fervor and the movement that Pollock seems to be making toward the literal, which is certainly how the generation of Frank Stella and Richard Serra saw it. However, whereas Stella seems in the late 1950s to be closing the door on certain possibilities, Twombly can be said to be opening the door on others.

One possibility that Twombly achieves is the ability to become other people through citation: his writing out of someone's name becomes an assertion of authorship. He becomes the author of the name that is written. Another is that all times and moments exist in the present. Twombly's first encounter with these ideas was at Black Mountain College, where he studied with the poet Charles Olson. Olson was influenced by Ezra Pound and his belief that all periods were accessible. Thus, one can link Pound and Twombly with Clemente and De Maria.

A painterly tradition informed by poetry is something that has been all but ignored by art historians, not to mention cultural theorists. However, for Clemente and De Maria the importance of Twombly rests in the poetic, rather than the purely formal. They aren't trying to extend his desiccated line. Instead, they are among the few artists of their generation, both in Italy and elsewhere, to recognize that Twombly's art points to two distinct possibilities: polymorphous fantasies and a world where past and present exist simultaneously. It is this side of Twombly, one that is both allusive and learned, both quoting and dreaming, that Clemente and De Maria are able to convincingly transmute into their own distinctive visions.

II.

Quite early in their respective careers, Francesco Clemente completed *Francesco Clemente Pinxit* (1980–81), and Nicola De Maria completed *Parole Cinesi* (1978–84), large, defining bodies of work that, in both cases, announced the presence of a fully formed sensibility. For while Clemente and De Maria may have been young artists chronologically, these works embodied a vision that was as complete as the one viewers encountered in Jasper Johns's first show at Leo Castelli in 1958. By defining, I mean that *Francesco Clemente Pinxit* and *Parole Cinesi* are complexly resonant, self-contained bodies of work that continue to cast an illuminating light on what the artists have subsequently gone on to do.

In these series, Clemente and De Maria invigorated as well as revitalized the difficult and challenging legacy of Arthur Rimbaud, who wrote "Je est un Autre" (I am Other). In doing so, they broadened our understanding of what is permissible in the field of painting and drawing, of the practice of art that many have denounced as being traditional or worse, irrelevant and obsolete. For by stating that one must "systematically derange" one's senses, that "I am Other," Rimbaud signaled a break with the history of the unified, lyric "I."

As Rimbaud grasped, the boundaries of one's being, one's self, were no longer fixed, like the borders one sees on a map. Rather, he understood that the boundaries of the self were both porous and in flux. His radical assertion, so important both in the arts and in the understanding of the self's relationship to reality, is central to understanding the work of both Clemente and De Maria. For in their work, what emerges is an "I" that is full of doubles and personae, that is both fragmented and boundless, that is both autobiographical and fictive, that is both present and absent. It is an "I" that is a conduit, a receiver of dreams: It registers in color and line, image and mark, what it hears and sees.

Done in gouache, and made up of twenty-four unbound sheets of antique paper, *Francesco Clemente Pinxit* is a book, complete with title page. "Francesco Clemente Pinxit" appears on the first sheet of paper, "pinxit" being a term meaning "painted (this)." Thus, the title reads, "Francesco Clemente painted this." It's both a claim of authorship and a sly comment on authorship, as Clemente worked with adolescent boys who were apprentices in a miniature-painting workshop in India. Working alongside the apprentices, he would describe particular images, which one of them would make in the style of an Indian miniature. In doing so, Clemente inhabits a style that is preestablished and not his own. What he does is introduce images that are new, possibilities which have not been used before. He transforms a well-defined historical tradition into a capacious appetite.

Of course, working with apprentices is a tradition that goes back to the medieval guild tradition and to the painting workshops that flourished throughout Italy during the Renaissance. In a sense, Clemente uses an ongoing Indian tradition to revitalize a moribund Italian one. At the same time, the gouaches mix together fantasy images of a man with a tree growing out of his groin, naked men with telescopes peering in from the sides of the composition, allusions to a soccer field, sexual and scatological scenes, dreamlike images of amputations.

One theme running through the work is power and the loss of power, gratification and the absence of it. This conflict between power and the loss of it is echoed in the work on a formal level. Who, we might ask, made it? Did Clemente make it, or did the apprentices make it? The answer is that neither could have made it alone, that it was a work that arose out of a decision to collaborate, which requires that one put aside one's ego. It is this putting aside of one's ego in order to make art that is central to Clemente's approach. Thus, we should remember that Clemente collaborated with Jean-Michel Basquiat and Andy Warhol on a series of paintings, as well as illustrated a number of poems by Allen Ginsberg and John Weiners. In 1986, he and Raymond Foye started Hanuman Books, which published more than fifty books by writers and artists such as Gregory Corso, Robert Creeley, Willem de Kooning, Henri Michaux, Cookie Mueller, Francis Picabia, and Patti Smith. It is worth noting that this distinguished list includes European and American writers, as well as artists from different generations.

The interiors of the block letters on the cover of *Francesco Clemente Pinxit* are decorated with repetitions of the simple, stylized image of a flower, while the letters themselves are arranged like those we might see on a movie marquee. By working within the constraints of a highly refined workshop style that has been refined over centuries, Clemente is able suppress his individualism. By using repeated patterns and block letters, Clemente subtly distances himself from the work. At the same time, because of the stylized settings and use of patterns, and because of its mixing together of non-Western and Western imagery, *Francesco Clemente Pinxit* strikes the viewer as an artifact from both a lost time and another world. The combination of sexual, scatological, and dreamlike images suggests that the book was made for private reasons by an artist named Francesco Clemente, rather than by a contemporary artist we call "Francesco Clemente." This sense that there is a *doppelganger* or double is one of the recurring preoccupations in Clemente's work, the self as both many and other. And, as *Francesco Clemente Pinxit* makes so palpably clear, the *doppelganger* inhabits an interior world, a dream space where the ego and superego surrender to the id, to that side of ourselves we all too often keep hidden from others and, worse, from ourselves. Clemente is unafraid of exploring his many selves, however disturbing they might be.

Nicola De Maria's definition of the self differs from Clemente's to the point that one could almost regard these two artists as going in opposite directions. For while Clemente's self seems fragmented, haunted, and chthonic, De Maria's self is various and infinite, on the point of disappearing into many others, as well as into the elemental world. Clemente's self becomes the Other, the Double, while De Maria's self seems to be many Others.

In *Parole Cinesi,* a large series of paintings and works on paper, De Maria writes the name of a classical Chinese poet-painter on each work. In the painting *Parole Cinesi Li Po, Tu Fu, Wang Wei* (1981), he writes all three names. And in the group of works on paper shown at the Kunsthaus Zurich (1985) and

Kunstmuseum Bonn (1986), the name of a seventeenth-century Chinese painter appears in large red letters on each sheet. In writing the names out in red, De Maria is consciously alluding to the Chinese classical tradition, where an artist signs his best work by using a seal of his name dipped in red ink.

Thus, *Parole Cinesi* is an extensive group of paintings and works on paper that has been only partially documented. The writing is casual and unhurried; and it usually occurs along or near the bottom edge. Within the composition, the name makes as strong a claim on our attention as the austere, sensual drawing of a plantlike form. Using a pictorial vocabulary that usually consists of one or two vertical lines from which a handful of lines extend, De Maria depicts a spare, plantlike form that evokes ideograms and signs. Here, the convincing power of De Maria's drawing becomes evident. We can read the drawing as an ideogram, linear abstraction, sign or symbol for a plant. Rather than belonging to one category, De Maria's drawing collapses these linguistic categories together, rendering them descriptively inadequate.

There are also different-sized dots and circles, sometimes concentrically arranged. These circles allude to flowers in bloom, as well as to light moving and pulsing. The world De Maria evokes is not static; it is an active, highly charged place. The marks can be made with pencil, paint, watercolor, or pastel. In a number of the works, a piece of torn paper that has been marked is attached to the larger paper. This joining suffuses the work with a sense of fragility and enduring strength. A bundle of pencil lines strikes us as being as delicate as the few bare stems it alludes to. The result is a work that is full of tenderness.

De Maria doesn't try to work in the style of a seventeenth-century Chinese artist. Rather, it's as if Li Sung, Li Shan, and others have been able to inhabit his work and practice, and, for a time, become him. Their signatures are evidence that they have made De Maria an instrument of their work.

In working this way, De Maria extends a little-known Italian tradition that originated in China. Guiseppe Castiglione (1688–1766) left Italy and arrived in China in 1715. His reason for going to China was to spread Christianity, but instead he became a painter who mastered the art of Chinese brush painting and was well received in the court of the emperor. He worked in China for fifty years and took on a Chinese name, Lang Shi-ning, which means "world peace." Castiglione's best paintings are of horses, where Chinese brushwork renders horses in a naturalistic setting. Castiglione's flawless synthesis of both Western and Eastern art is original and unmistakable, and his oeuvre forms a unique chapter in the history of art.

Without ever having gone to China, De Maria achieves something equally original and unmistakable. The fluidity of De Maria's vocabulary, and the fact that the lines never stop being lines, even as they become images, signs, and symbols, are comparable to how we think of the Chinese ideogram. We both read and see the lines in De Maria's work. And yet, even as we do so, what distinguishes them from their inspiration is the oscillating color. Thus, *Parole Cinesi* consists of works we see, read, and engage with physically. In using paint, words, and collage, De Maria addresses different ways we apprehend reality (seeing, reading, touching). And he does so on a scale that is both intimate and personal.

In *Yen Tz'u-Yu, Pittore Della Cina* (1984), for example, there is the writing, the drawing, and the physicality of the white paint. Is the white paint, its fulsome drops, blossoms blowing in a flurry of wind or large flakes of soft snow? Both, I would say, and thus a world that is imagined to be real becomes as real as one's imagination. It is an idyllic world, a world to be both named (made visible) and protected, which is exactly what De Maria does. What is remarkable about this act of naming is that the artist does so by becoming other artists, by losing himself in their spirits.

Assembled as a book, which accompanied an exhibition of *Parole Cinesi* in Zurich and Bonn, the individual works become a gathering of visual poems by seventeenth-century Chinese artists, an act of preservation and recovery by an archivist, somebody working anonymously in the great library that is the infinite present. Time and timelessness have been made to intersect. As De Maria has repeatedly made clear throughout his career, art is not to be divided into past and present, then and now. Rather, it is all part of what the poet Frank O'Hara called the "living situation."

III.

For many years Clemente has done portraits in watercolor of friends and acquaintances, people he admires. In 1983, shortly after meeting Allen Ginsberg, he and the poet collaborated on *White Shroud,* a poem in which the poet dreams that his mother didn't die in a mental institution, but is living on the streets of the Bronx, homeless. Ginsberg handwrote the poem on separate sheets of paper, while Clemente used ink, pencil, and watercolor to transform these sheets into the pages of an illuminated manuscript.

In *Story of My Country* (1990), Clemente directed an Orissan miniaturist to depict scenes from different mythologies and countries, a world made up of fragments. Each of the eighteen sheets evokes a self-contained narrative, a worldview. The echoes and mirroring remind us that even in our separateness there are parallels and joinings, events common to us all.

De Maria has done groups of watercolors, often on very small sheets of paper. A series of forty watercolors done in July and August of 1978 were exhibited nearly a decade later, in 1986, accompanied by a book *(Nicola de Maria: 40 Ladroni)* that reproduces them all. Along with the reproductions are the artist's notes from that period. A delicate body of work, a work of delicacy–one senses that De Maria's art is one of offerings, of gifts made to the world.

On the other end of the scale from their intimately scaled works are installations, large rooms that the artists have transformed into compelling sites (sights). In 1981–82, Clemente worked on a series of large oil paintings, *The Fourteen Stations.* In *The Fourteen Stations VIII,* he depicted himself lying naked in the upper part of the painting. Five different shoes and slippers are scattered across him, from his head to his knee. In the foreground, three large-eared mice (or are they rats?) are cavorting, unafraid. To varying degrees, the artist's awareness of mortality, his seemingly morbid preoccupation with decay, and his honest sense of the polymorphic nature of one's imagination have all been brought into play. We are both in and out of paradise, both in and out of our bodies.

A room that is a rich, luminous blue, a deep blue, the blue of the sky before dawn when the sun, still below the horizon, is making its way steadily upward. It is the hour of solitude and dreams. A few paintings have been placed high up on the wall. Another room, the blue more misty, punctuated by red circles whose edges are dissolving, a suitcase on the floor, near the wall. De Maria has painted the suitcase white, the white of clouds and pillows and sheets. The suitcase can be opened or closed. It can contain a small, exquisite drawing or a painting can rest on it, while leaning against a wall. Again, we can see this room in counterpoint to Clemente's *The Fourteen Stations*. For while the body in all its manifestations is Clemente's recurring subject, De Maria's seems to be about that place where the artist vanishes, leaving behind physical proof of his vision or dream. Thus, a painting for Jack Kerouac is a tondo placed below a window overlooking the landscape. The round painting or steering wheel has allowed Kerouac to vanish into the world outside.

Both Clemente and De Maria are dreamers whose work suggests that the plenitude and variousness of the world have only been glimpsed, that there is always more to discover. This is the journey on which each of them set out over two decades ago.

IV.

I want to leave Clemente and De Maria with the final words. In their statements both artists mix together the senses. Is it simply coincidence? Or is synthesthesia a trait that is shared by poet-painters, by visionaries?

In an interview with Donald Kuspit, Clemente said: "I am a believer in the voice of each level, the voice of the place in the self. This voice comes before poetry, painting, music."[4] De Maria has described himself as "someone who writes a poem with fingers full of colors."[5]

NOTES

1. "The Other Tradition" is the title of a poem by John Ashbery, which appeared in *Houseboat Days* (New York: Viking, 1977).

2. “Francesco Clemente,” a fugue for Alighiero E. Boetti, in *Alighiero E Boetti,* exhibition catalog (New York: Gagosian Gallery, 2001), p. 69. In an interview with Louise Neri, Clemente stated that he met Boetti in Rome in 1973.

3. In a fax dated Sept. 11, 2002, and sent to the author, De Maria states that he met Mario and Marisa Merz in Turin in 1977.

4. “Clemente explores Clemente,” *Contemporanea* (New York) 2, no. 7 (Oct. 1989): p. 41.

5. *Domus* no. 640 (June 1983).

Open Books

"Emblems for Robert Duncan," by Jess

I.

Had Jorge Luis Borges been a visual artist, his work might have borne a strong resemblance to Jess's "paste-ups." In Borges's fabulist tale "The Garden of Forking Paths," Albert (one of two seemingly interchangeable characters) describes a novel:

> The Garden of Forking Paths is an incomplete, but not false, image of the universe as Ts'ui Pen conceived it. In contrast to Newton and Schopenhauer, your ancestor did not believe in uniform, absolute time. He believed in an infinite series of times, in a growing, dizzying net of divergent, convergent, and parallel times, which approached one another, forked, broke off, or were unaware of one another for centuries, embraces all possibilities of time.[1]

Borges's speculation about time can be read as a fitting description of the dense intricate network Jess carefully structures in each of his paste-ups. What Jess and Borges articulate with incredible suppleness is a complex labyrinth of imaginative possibilities. Thus, Jess's paste-ups can also be seen as the visual equivalent of Borges's imaginary novel; like "The Garden of Forking Paths" (both the story and the imaginary novel within the story), the paste-ups are formed out of a "dizzying net of divergent, convergent, and parallel" images which em-

---

Exhibition catalog, San Jose Museum of Art (1990).

body a wide range of associations and open-ended narrative possibilities.

By structuring the discrete images in ways that suggest larger abstract shapes, Jess achieves a state of implied, multidirectional movement, as well as conveys flux and metamorphosis. The shapes define both a fluid spatial continuum and disjunctive assemblies. It seems likely that while he was studying with Clyfford Still, he became familiar with large fluid shapes as a structuring device in gestural painting. It is his construction of a fluid structural form made up of distinct images that distinguishes the paste-ups from Max Ernst's collages, where images were assembled within an illusionistic space, often of a room.

In speaking about his paste-ups, Jess has stated:

> I wanted to be able to look at a canvas and read something happening like a novel or adventure story. There are many stories in the Paste-Ups, not just a story. There is a network of stories there and anybody can pick out any story they choose.[2]

As one of Borges's characters says:

> We do not exist in the majority of these times; in some you exist, and not I; in others I, and not you; in others, both of us. In the present one, which a favorable fate has granted me, you have arrived at my house; in another, while walking across the garden, you found me dead; in another I utter these same words, but I am a mistake, a ghost.[3]

A ghost story or a ghost telling a story? In Jess's paste-ups, identity and context are conditional to change. He enlarges the narrative from the singular and heroic to the multiple and democratic. This undoing of linear narrative and closed plot causes the viewer to become the author (the teller of tales) and the artist to become the reader, the one who removes these images from their previous contexts, and, discerning the emergence of open-ended possibilities, uses them to establish a multidirectional fictive space. As Jess has stated: "The collage takes over; it becomes the maker and I the instrument."[4]

II.

Jess (the artist dropped his surname years ago) was born in Long Beach, California, in 1923, Initially, he studied to become a radiochemist, and, for a time in the mid-1940s, he worked on the Manhattan Project in Oak Ridge, Tennessee, and was involved with the production of plutonium. In 1948, after completing the requirements for a bachelor's of science in radiochemistry at the California Institute of Technology (Pasadena), he began working on the Hanford Project (again involved with the production of plutonium) in Washington. As an antidote to his involvement with science and the development of potentially destructive forces, Jess began taking art classes on the weekends.

In 1949, he abruptly changed the direction of his life and enrolled in the California School of Fine Arts (now the San Francisco Art Institute). Under the directorship of Douglas MacAgy, who began his tenure in 1945, the school had been able to put together a faculty that included David Park, Richard Diebenkorn, Edward Corbett, Hassel Smith, and Clyfford Still. This atmosphere was not to last. In 1951, MacAgy was replaced, and many of the faculty and students, including Jess, left. It was during this time that Jess met and formed a lifelong relationship with the poet Robert Duncan (1919–88). It was for him that Jess made these fourteen paste-ups, collectively titled *Emblems for Robert Duncan.* In Jess's words, they were "made in love and remembrance," and are meant to be included in the seven volumes of Duncan's complete writings which are to eventually be published by the University of California Press.[5] In order to tune the direction of the composition of the paste-ups, Jess read through all of Duncan's writings.

III.

There are a number of reasons why Jess became interested in the possibilities of collage. Shortly after he began his formal art education, he became dissatisfied with his own fledgling attempts at Action painting, as well as realized that he was deeply attracted to the possible uses of representational imagery. At the same time, he knew that he had come to drawing late and that it was unlikely that he would master this medium fast enough to become something more than a beginner. Collage offered him an alternative to drawing:

> They (the Paste-Ups) do in a hurry what takes me a long time to do. I didn't start out as a child or young man to learn the skills with the hand and eye. When I was twenty-eight and becoming an artist, I no longer had the ability to learn these things. I don't have the assiduous nature of an older person who can learn his way. What my mind wanted to see happen would require skills that I could not possibly use. Therefore, I had to use images that had already been made for me. They came and asked to be used in the way I wanted to. So collages were the sensible answer to the problem.[6]

Formally, Jess began making collages as a response to his own lack of technical expertise. However, the use of collage was not solely a formal solution; it also enabled him to gain access to the vast domain of printed media, and, beyond that, his own imaginative and transformative powers.

Borges's tale "The Tower of Babel" begins: "The universe (which others call the library) is composed of an indefinite and perhaps infinite number of hexagonal galleries, with vast air shafts between, surrounded by very low railings."[7] For Borges and Jess, the world (the place where one glimpses aspects of his or her own identity) is what exists in books. Simultaneously specific and metaphorical, it exists in a relentless state of permutation.

IV.

Each of the fourteen black-and-white paste-ups is a tondo. The circular shape evokes portraiture, cyclical time, a bubble or convex mirror, a self-contained world. Jess repeatedly structures the tondo into a sphere-like realm, suggesting that there is a world that is parallel to the one we inhabit. Consequently, the paste-ups evoke a realm like one finds in glass paperweights, where an entire scene is taking place. The difference is that Jess's scenes are abutted against and within other scenes, so that one's focus keeps changing. We see these worlds, but we can neither enter nor annex their domains. Through this format, Jess addresses Robert Duncan's life and death. In their connections, echoes, and acts of remembering, Jess's *Emblems for Robert Duncan* parallels Shelley's "Adonais," a magisterial elegy for John Keats in which the poet tries through language to bring his friend back to life.

During the past forty years, Jess has accumulated and cataloged an immense library of visual items. For these fourteen paste-ups, he selected images from a wide range of sources, including modern paintings, world history, literature, nineteenth-century steel engravings, scientific journals, personal history, mythology, old master paintings, news photographs, and children's storybooks. Through a process of moving and adjusting each fragment, its relationship to other fragments and images, the artist constructs a space in which an image fragment can function as both local event and part of an overall flow. The viewer is constantly connecting one image to another. In doing so, a multilayered, multifocused story radiates out from each event. Once we visually engage with a paste-up, we are in what Borges called "the garden of forking paths."

Jess's paste-ups have been aptly described as a "kaleidoscopic matrix of possible focuses."[8] Within his carefully tuned, nonhierarchical compositions, every image becomes equally important. The world they conjure up is a network of criss-crossing, interpenetrating realities. None of them is more actual than any other. Bees, for example, are winged insects, gatherers of nectar, members of a highly structured social order, beings who communicate through dance. In the Ptolemaic empire, beekeeping was an organized production, which was both taxed and regulated. Aristotle and Virgil are among the Greek and Latin authors who wrote about bees. Maeterlinck wrote eloquently about bees. Architects such as Antoni Gaudi and Peter Behrens saw the beehive as a paradigm of a utopian community.

In the third paste-up, Jess has placed the image of a bee just above the center of the tondo. Below it and rising from the tondo's round bottom edge is the image of a smiling boy holding a book. A white rabbit floats between the book and the boy's face. In 1967, White Rabbit Press published a children's book by Duncan entitled *The Cat and the Blackbird* (1967), for which Jess did the illustrations. Jutting out of the boy's head is the profile of a young man who is wearing a crown of laurel leaves (the classical image of a poet) and looking at an owl. The Romans believed the owl was a sign of bad luck, while the Greeks thought of it as a benevolent sign, and linked its presence to Athena, goddess of wisdom.

In his book *Letters,* Duncan included the poem "An Owl Is an Only Bird of Poetry," which contains the following lines:

> The vowels are physical
> corridors of the imagination
> emitting passionately
> breaths of flame. In a poem
> the vowels appear like
> the flutterings of an owl
> caught in a web and give
> aweful intimations of eternal life.[9]

Duncan's expansion of the word "awful" into "aweful" reminds us that the word originally meant "full of reverential fear."

The owl is resting on the lower branch of a tree that stretches around the upper half of the tondo, forming an archway or proscenium. On the right side, almost directly opposite the owl, is a statue wielding an axe. The tree connects the owl to the bee and the statue. The viewer might deduce both a beginning and an ending, or one kind of ending (night) juxtaposed with another (statue). The bee and rabbit are echoing images of fecundity. Thus, images evoking the time of day, season, youth, and early manhood are fitted together, like pieces in a jigsaw puzzle.

Through carefully considered choice and placement, Jess encourages various and seemingly contradictory narratives to branch out, echo, and return. Placement is his way of establishing a continuum between identity and context. The result is a visual tapestry. Like James Joyce's *Finnegans Wake,* one of Duncan's and Jess's favorite books, every image seems, like an ouroboros, to circle back on itself.[10] This sense of return, of images being able to feed off and sustain the images around them, to become an instance in a vibrant field, recalls Duncan's description of the practice of poetry: "To write at all is to dwell in the illusion of language, the rapture of communication that comes as we surrender our troubled individual isolated experiences to the communal consciousness."[11]

Duncan's belief in both the "rapture of communication" and "communal consciousness" suggests another reason why Jess chose the image of a bee. Both artist and poet are bees, productive members of society. Alliteration permits the viewer still another entrance into the third paste-up. Birds, bard, boy, branch, blossom, bunny, and bee—the sound all these words share is both the letter *b* and the word "bee." Both as sound (word) and image, *b* ("be" and "bee") seems to be one of the generating principles of the composition.

Might not Jess be suggesting that in being itself there exists both the desire and the rapture of communication? And, in making the connection between sound and image, isn't the artist also reminding us that poetry is both a written and a spoken art, and that it aspires to the condition of music? In this regard, the viewer can see the third paste-up as a hive in which images and sounds mingle together, even as they dance around each other.

Constructed out of hexagons, Borges's universe (library) is based on the paradigm of the hive, the "indefinite and perhaps infinite" structure of "communal consciousness." Jess's library, the source of his images, is the continually growing domain of all printed matter. "The world," as Stéphane Mallarmé wrote, "exists to end up in a book." But what is in a book (or a section of a hive), Jess might reply, is living matter; it is the sounds we make in order to communicate.

V.

In the seventh paste-up, a photograph of Robert Duncan (in profile) is surrounded by images of Dante, William Shakespeare, Walt Whitman, and Homer, among others. In the eleventh paste-up, a photograph of Duncan as a young man (full face) has been placed near the middle of the tondo. Among the faces clustered around him, one notices Charles Olson, Charles Baudelaire, James Joyce, Edith Sitwell, and Gertrude Stein. Nourished by the work of others, as well as both extending and defining tradition, the poet is part of a larger community. Within this context, the image of the bee gains further resonance.

The largest image in the eleventh paste-up is a profile view of Ezra Pound. The white outline of an ancient sailing ship has been juxtaposed against his thick dark hair. The ancient and modern commingled in a single figure, whose audacious, learned work inspired Duncan and other poets of his generation. The conjunction of classical and modern, the sailing ship and Pound's profile, underscores the fact that Ulysses, the hero of Homer's epic, is the reigning spirit in the first canto of Pound's modern epic, *The Cantos.*

At the same time, Pound's self—the one that is represented in and through his writings—is made up of other selves, which have been articulated by earlier writers. Pound wrote in the personae of Chinese poets, Provençal troubadours, historical figures, and mythological beings. *Personae,* we also remember, is the title of one of Pound's books.

As a poet who believed Greek myths and children's stories were equally important sources for poetry, Duncan ranged far and wide in his use of different material. An erudite man, he called himself a "derivative" poet because he believed that he was working within a tradition that extended back to Dante and the troubadours, and, beyond that, to Pindar and Homer. Duncan wasn't focused on being original, but on learning how to make use of that which tradition had given him. For Duncan, reading and writing were deeply entwined activities. Jess, himself a deep reader, uses the world of found images to disclose imaginative possibilities to the viewer. Both men believe that art and literature are living traditions made up of the larger cycles of birth and death. For them, the poet and artist are figures of renewal.

VI.

The image of children dancing in a circle appears in the second and tenth paste-ups. This image, which is also a motif in Duncan's poem "Often I am Permitted to Return to a Meadow," underscores the cyclical nature of time.[12] It reminds both reader and viewer alike that each of us exists within a pattern (passing) of time. The children both celebrate and learn this fact by reciting the words of the nursery rhyme "Ring around the Rosie."

In the second paste-up, the word "sing" (contained within a heart-like shape) has been affixed to the right-hand page of an open book. The book is held aloft by a right hand emerging from the bottom of the tondo. Also emerging from the bottom of the tondo is a left hand, which is affixing a heart (containing the image of a book full of musical notes) to the open book's left-hand page. While Jess is equating the making of the paste-up with singing, he has also placed the images of the hands so that the unseen arms extend into the viewer's space; we are simultaneously holding the book aloft, singing, and making the paste-up. Above the book, a circle of children dance, round and round, celebrating the nature of time, its passing and return.

Out of death and personal loss, Jess has fashioned a series of paste-ups whose theme is constant renewal. Images of celebration and lamentation are woven together through this ever-changing tapestry of specific visual events.

NOTES

1. Jorge Luis Borges, "The Garden of Forking Paths," in *Labyrinths: Selected Stories and Other Writings,* trans. Donald A. Yates and James E. Irby (New York: New Directions, 1964), p. 28.

2. Michael Auping, "Jess, Paste-Ups (and Assemblies) 1951–1983," in *Jess, Paste-Ups (and Assemblies) 1951–1983* (Sarasota: John and Mabel Ringling Museum of Art, 1983), p. 12.

3. Borges, "The Garden," p. 28.

4. Robert M. Murdock, "Introduction," in *Jess: Translations, Salvages, and Paste-Ups* (Dallas: Dallas Museum of Fine Arts, 1977), n.p.

5. In conversation with the author, San Francisco, CA, Sept. 24, 1989.

6. Auping, "Jess," p. 11.

7. Borges, "The Tower of Babel," in *Labyrinths,* p. 51.

8. Auping, "Jess," p. 12.

9. Robert Duncan, "xxvii, An Owl Is an Only Bird of Poetry," in *Letters* (Highlands, NC: Jargon, 1958), n.p.

10. An "ouroboros" is defined as a "gnostic and alchemical symbol of the snake devouring its own tail. It symbolizes the cycles of life and Nature, the fusion of opposites, and the transcendence of duality." See Nevill Drury, *Dictionary of Mysticism and the Occult* (San Francisco: Harper and Row, 1985), p. 203.

11. Robert Duncan, *A Caterpillar Anthology*, ed. Clayton Eshleman (Garden City, NY: Doubleday, 1971), p. 62.

12. Robert Duncan, "Often I Am Permitted to Return to a Meadow," in *The Opening of the Field* (New York: Grove Press. 1960), p. 7.